Used personally or in a grou
to live more fully as a disciple of Jesus. ✣ **LAUREN HANLEY CSJ,** *coordinator of spiritual formation, St. Frances De Chantal Parish, Wantagh, NY*

Jim Philipps has, once more, found a gentle way to challenge us to be smarter about what we say we believe. The Scripture selection is wide and provocative, and Jim's questions make me nervous—in a good way.
✣ **ALICE CAMILLE,** *author of* **God's Word Is Alive** *and* **This Transforming Word**

This book is an excellent opportunity for individuals or parish groups to discuss how we can live as disciples of Jesus in our society.
✣ **SHEILA BROWNE, RSM,** *RCIA director, St. Edward's Parish, Syosset, NY*

I found the meditations to be challenging and insightful. The questions are open-ended and thought-provoking. Jim clearly understands the struggle to be a follower of Christ in the world today.
✣ **KAREN MUSICARO, LCSW,** *adjunct instructor, Molloy College*

Where was this book when I was discerning between staying in my corporate job or taking a position offered to me by the church?
✣ **SUZANNE RICHARDS,** *pastoral associate, Christ the King Church, Commack, NY*

Jim Philipps has many years of experience teaching about social justice. He is a dynamic teacher and has facilitated many retreats and prayer groups. All of that experience comes into play in these twenty meditations. An enjoyable, meditative, and practical book!
✣ **CLARICE SPICA CURRY, MA, LCSW,** *adjunct assistant professor of Theology, St. John's University; social worker and president of the board of directors, Bethany House of Nassau County, Inc.*

The meditations in this book are worthwhile for everyone, especially those Christians whose work lives are focused on business endeavors intended to create wealth. ✣ **FRANK DELLAQUILA, CFO**

I love the format of this book: Scripture passage, reflection, questions that provide an opportunity for dialogue, growth, and change. The closing prayers are a nice ending to some heavy-duty soul searching.
✣ **CYNTHIA GARCIA,** *chairperson, religion department, Cathedral High School, Rockville Center, NY*

DEDICATION

To all those who,
by word, example, and prayer
have helped me to see that
Who We Are
is so vastly more important than
What We Have

TWENTY-THIRD PUBLICATIONS
One Montauk Avenue, Suite 200
New London, CT 06320
(860) 437-3012 or (800) 321-0411
www.twentythirdpublications.com

Cover photo: ©Shutterstock / kamon_saejueng

ISBN: 978-1-62785-355-2
Library of Congress Control Number: 2017960973
Printed in the U.S.A.

 A division of Bayard, Inc.

James Philipps

YOUR MONEY

— or —

YOUR LIFE

20 sessions on **faith**, finances
and the choices we make

TWENTY-THIRD
PUBLICATIONS
twentythirdpublications.com

CONTENTS

ACKNOWLEDGMENTS   *vi*

INTRODUCTION   1

MEDITATION ONE
How well do I discern what belongs to Caesar
and what belongs to God?   6

MEDITATION TWO
Is my attitude toward wealth a Christian attitude?   11

MEDITATION THREE
Is my attitude toward wealth informed by faith?   16

MEDITATION FOUR
Am I truly generous?   21

MEDITATION FIVE
Where is my treasure?   26

MEDITATION SIX
Am I aware of my abundance?   31

MEDITATION SEVEN
Who am I stepping over?   37

MEDITATION EIGHT
Is my wealth too "sticky"?   42

MEDITATION NINE
Am I losing my sense of solidarity with the poor?   46

MEDITATION TEN
Am I a sheep or a goat?   51

MEDITATION ELEVEN
Am I with Mary and the poor?   56

MEDITATION TWELVE
Is my concern for the poor real or reality TV?   61

MEDITATION THIRTEEN
If given the choice, "your money or your life,"
which would I choose?   66

MEDITATION FOURTEEN
How aware am I of the existence of Structural Sin?   70

MEDITATION FIFTEEN
Am I a cheerful giver?   75

MEDITATION SIXTEEN
Am I "the man"(or "the woman")?   80

MEDITATION SEVENTEEN
Do I use the goods of this world to advance
the Kingdom?   85

MEDITATION EIGHTEEN
Do I "pray away" my obligation to the poor?   91

MEDITATION NINETEEN
Am I letting my desire for material gain
destroy my Sabbath?   96

MEDITATION TWENTY
Am I building a legacy or a useless tower?   101

ACKNOWLEDGMENTS

I am most grateful to Diane Vella, the director of adult faith formation at St. Bernard's parish in Levittown, New York, and to the pastor, Father Ralph Sommer, and the parishioners of St. Bernard's for giving me the opportunity to "road test" these meditations in a prayerful community setting.

Thank you to Trish Vanni for helping me to articulate the idea for this book more clearly and for shepherding that idea through the early stages of the publication process.

Thanks to Dan Connors and Dan Smart for all of their feedback, advice, and guidance about how to make this book both readable and marketable.

Thanks as always to Kerry Moriarty for her continuing help in finding answers to all of the various and sundry questions I ask.

Thanks to Michelle Gerstel and Jeff McCall for all of their efforts in preparing this book for its publication.

I am continually grateful to my wife, Rosalie, and to my children for their support and love and honest feedback on my work and on my attempts, imperfect as they are, to practice what I preach.

Finally, thanks to all of those who see the inherent tensions between capitalism and Christianity and who willingly enter that breach courageously and lovingly in order to really understand what it means to be "in the world but not of the world."

INTRODUCTION

When the idea for this book was suggested to me by my editors at Twenty-Third Publications, two stories immediately came to mind. The first happened about twenty years ago during the time I was teaching a course entitled "Morality and the Marketplace" at St. John's University in New York City. One of my best students was a man who owned his own ice cream truck. At the conclusion of our class, which was somewhere around noon, he would head off to work. One day he came up to me at the end of class and told me he was going to have to withdraw. I was really disappointed to hear this, and I asked him if he was having any trouble with the subject matter of the Morality and the Marketplace class or if I perhaps had done or said something to upset him. He assured me that this wasn't the case and that in fact he enjoyed the class. His problem was an economic one. In his absence, a rival driver had begun to horn in on his territory!

The second story took place only a few years ago. I was attending Sunday Mass at my parish, and the celebrant gave a homily focusing on the difference between honest and dishonest use of wealth. During the course of his remarks, he pointed out that as we reflected upon the financial disaster rooted in the default of so many home mortgages (which came to be known as the Great Recession), we needed to recognize that some of the responsibility rested with the improper handling of wealth on Wall Street. At the end of the Mass, I went over to him to thank him for touching on this topic. (Rarely do I hear topics that touch on the social justice teachings of the church, other than the right to life, addressed from the pulpit.) He laughed and told me that a man he had spoken to just before me had quite a different take. That man asked him a question: What right did he have to comment on the financial practices of the business world when the institutional church has so many problems of its own?

Both these stories help explain why the meditations in this book—which focus both on proper attitudes toward, and proper use of, our wealth—are so important. The struggle we face in trying to make a living within this highly competitive and uncertain economy often compromises the time we have available to truly understand the subtle ways our call to follow Christ influences not just the career paths we choose but the day-to-day decisions we make in our economic lives. Even in the seemingly halcyon business of selling ice cream to children, such intense competition exists that my student was forced to choose between maintaining his livelihood and learning how to pursue that livelihood in a manner more consistent with the mind of Christ. Furthermore, the long history of Catholic moral teaching focusing on individual sin has created within many of us the blind spot exemplified by the man in the second story.

While he could see with some clarity the moral failings of the institutional church, he could not imagine that Jesus might have anything to say about the way Wall Street bankers, traders, and financiers manage the wealth of so many Americans who depend on their integrity, professionalism, and empathy. Our commitment to Christian discipleship is defined much more by what we do from Monday to Friday than it is by what we do on Sunday. And so much of what we do from Monday to Friday involves the decisions we make to accumulate, save, and share our wealth.

When the social justice teaching of the church calls upon us to be good stewards, when Jesus says that it is easier for a camel to get through the eye of a needle than for a rich man to get to heaven, an essential point is being made about wealth. I can easily visualize the camel getting stuck! Wealth—the sum total of all of our worldly possessions, as well as the power and influence we are able to exert in the public square—is inherently "sticky." In and of itself, wealth is not bad. If we are good stewards of the material blessings which God has bestowed upon us, we can do much good with them—for our families, our world, and even for ourselves. Yet attachments to wealth form so easily and so subtly; I can think of countless things in my life which once seemed to be luxuries but now appear to be necessities. How about you? (My list is long indeed.)

We can so easily forget that no one really succeeds on his or her own. All of our hard work could just as easily have come to nothing but for the love and sacrifices of others, some of whom we know personally, many of whom we do not. And perhaps most dangerous of all, the more wealthy one becomes, the easier it is to lose touch with those who are crushed by injustice and to lose the motivation he or she once had to change things. (It is awfully difficult to change a system, even an unjust one, from which one has benefited.)

The purpose of these meditations, all based on scriptural passages pertaining to wealth and stewardship, is to invite you to think deeply and prayerfully—both individually and with others. Each meditation follows the same basic process. (See the appendix for a more specific breakdown if you need it.) Begin each meditation with a quieting exercise, followed by attentive and prayerful listening to the Scripture reading. A brief written reflection follows the passage, which can be read aloud or silently. (If the written reflection is read aloud, I would encourage the leader to use only those parts of it which he or she feels are necessary to clarify or emphasize key points in the reading. Sometimes less is more.)

Next comes a time of quiet prayer during which each person can use the discussion questions to guide their musings. After sufficient time has passed, the group can use any or all of the questions as the jumping off point for a more informed and honest exchange. At the conclusion of the meeting time, the group might use the "Going forward" statements as a means of setting individual and communal goals to be carried forward until the next meeting time and beyond. Each session concludes with a brief closing prayer.

Making significant changes in our lifestyles is never easy. These times of prayer, however, can really help. Deep within our hearts, we know the difference between self-care and selfishness. Allow the Holy Spirit to transform your heart and mind just as the Spirit transforms the bread and wine into the living flesh and blood of Christ during the Eucharistic Prayer. The prophet Elijah did not meet God in the earthquake or the howling wind but in the "sheer silence" (1 Kings 19:11–13).

Take your time—these meditations could easily be spread out over the course of a year. Feel free to pray them in any order that seems right. Finally, remember that everything in this book is intended as a starting point, not a final destination. Use what helps, set aside what doesn't, and never be afraid to go "off road" and take the meditation in a different direction if the Spirit so moves you. It's often been said that the key to success is showing up; this is certainly true in the case of prayer. In my experience, God always does the rest.

IMPORTANT NOTE **FOR FACILITATORS**

You can feel confident that the meditations in this book are based
solidly upon the Scriptures and the social justice teaching of the
church. This does not necessarily mean, however, that the group
participants will be fully cognizant of this. Despite a tradition of
social justice teaching going back to the earliest days of the church,
and with a particular emphasis on the application of that teaching
to the economic complexities of the modern world dating from the
end of the nineteenth century, the catechesis many adult Catholics
have received on social justice is mostly limited to the right to life
principle as it pertains particularly to abortion and a recognition that
discipleship includes a commitment to charitable giving of time, talent,
and treasure. The idea that the demands of social justice also require
recognizing ways in which our lifestyles and day-to-day economic
decisions might promote or cause us to participate in social and
economic injustice, therefore, will be a difficult one for many to accept.

A great deal of patience, a commitment to making everyone feel
welcome, and an overall willingness to show Christian charity on
the part of all is essential. It is especially crucial, however, that the
facilitator sets a tone that encourages a prayerful and fruitful dialogue
that recognizes potential tensions in the room and intentionally calls
upon the Holy Spirit as a mediator. Such prayerful discernment
makes room for a wide variety of points of view but holds firmly to
the teaching of the church. In this way, any potential conflict can be
defused and such tensions that do arise can be transformed from
destructive to creative. (A sense of humor helps a great deal as well!)

Always keep in mind that God is not a capitalist, not a socialist,
not a communist, not a Democrat, not a Republican, not a
libertarian. God, of course, is the ultimate Independent!

How well do I discern what belongs to Caesar and what belongs to God?

So they watched him and sent spies who pretended to be honest, in order to trap him by what he said, so as to hand him over to the jurisdiction and authority of the governor. So they asked him, "Teacher, we know that you are right in what you say and teach, and you show deference to no one, but teach the way of God in accordance with truth. Is it lawful for us to pay taxes to the emperor, or not?" But he perceived their craftiness and said to them, "Show me a denarius. Whose head and whose title does it bear?" They said, "The emperor's." He said to them, "Then give to the emperor the things that are the emperor's, and to God the things that are God's."

+ LUKE 20:20–26

After many years in the classroom I can affirm from personal experience that there really are no stupid questions. There are, however, inauthentic questions. The purpose of a question is to seek greater truth, both in small (When is the homework assignment due?) and large (What is the meaning of life?) ways. Some questions that appear to be seeking clarification and understanding are, in fact, intended to deceive or manipulate. This Scripture reading makes clear that this is exactly the kind of question Jesus' enemies are asking. They "pretended to be honest, in order to trap him" by asking this question: "Is it lawful for us to pay taxes to the emperor, or not?"

Jesus lived in a time when Palestine was a province of the Roman Empire. While the Romans exhibited great tolerance when it came to religious practices, they made no allowance for political dissent; the emperor's authority was beyond question. The crucifixion of Jesus was by no means unique. During the Roman occupation, it is likely that thousands of Jews were crucified, mostly on the charge of treason.

By means of their question, Jesus' enemies think that they have set a foolproof trap. If Jesus says that the people should not pay their taxes, then he can be charged with sedition and handed over to the authorities to be executed. If he says the people should pay their taxes, his enemies can accuse him of being a Roman sympathizer, like Zacchaeus the tax collector, thus marking him as an enemy of the people. Either way, it would seem, they have him.

Jesus' answer is brilliant. Holding a coin bearing the emperor's image, he says, "Then give to the emperor the things that are the emperor's, and to God the things that are God's." On the surface, this answer seems to be an acknowledgment of the emperor's power, thus keeping Jesus on the right side of the law. Yet in the very act of making a distinction between *Things that Belong to the Emperor* and *Things that Belong to God*, Jesus is subtly engaging in subversion. The Romans understood no such distinction;

the emperor was the Great Bridge (*pontifex maximus*) who interceded with the gods on behalf of the people and who would join their exalted ranks upon his death. *Everything* belonged to Caesar, including the ability to influence the spiritual destinies of the people. With his response, Jesus puts the emperor in his place by making it clear that there is an entire spiritual realm—we call it the Kingdom of God—over which the emperor has no authority whatsoever.

Jesus' response invites us to think deeply. Where is the boundary between Caesar and God in our lives? Do we buy into the common superficial answer—"from Monday through Friday, I work for Caesar to earn a decent living, and on Sunday morning I belong to God"? If so, we aren't giving much to God at all. To what extent does what we profess to believe on Sunday mornings—our recognition of our failures to love our sisters and brothers as we should, our promise to make Jesus the center of our lives, the call to love without limits, as Jesus does—make its way into our work week? When we make the various economic decisions we need to make in the business world, how much are those decisions influenced by our values?

I know a man who works for an advertising firm not too far from Newtown, Connecticut. A short time after the massacre of twenty children and six teachers at the hands of a delusional young man with an assault rifle, the firm held a meeting to consider whether or not they should take on an account with a gun manufacturer. It was his clear sense that this deal went beyond the bounds of what Caesar had the right to ask, given the circumstances, that gave this man the courage to voice his strong objections to the proposal.

What do we see when we look at our home lives? Our choices of entertainment? Our commitment to our children? In an effort to keep Caesar happy, are we depriving our families of time with us they need and have a right to expect? Are we depriving ourselves of the joys of family life? Where is the line between necessary compromise with Caesar and selling out God to Caesar? How much of Caesar's coinage goes to healthy and wholesome pursuits, and how many of our dollars support lifestyle choices that are not really consistent with gospel values?

No one would deny the importance of family vacations and providing for the real needs of our loved ones and ourselves. Yet are we also concerned for the needs of those outside of our families? Do we make conscious choices to give a portion of what we earn to the needs of our parish and our community and to worthy charities, or is our giving limited to a few crumbs left on the table as an afterthought?

Upon deeper reflection, Jesus' "simple" answer leads us into a fuller consideration of the complicated ways Caesar and God are intertwined in our lives. Such reflection will inevitably force us to wrestle with a fundamental question: Is God or Caesar in charge? In our attempts to answer that question, it helps to remember not whose image is on a coin but in whose image we were made.

FOR REFLECTION *and* **DISCUSSION**

1. In my working life, what is the line between compromise and selling out? Have I crossed it recently?

2. On a scale of 1 to 10, with 1 being a complete disconnect and 10 being total harmony, how well do I incorporate the values I profess on Sunday in my day-to-day economic, political, and social life?

3. As a citizen, how is my faith influencing the choices I make when I vote? As a participant in the political life of my community?

4. Have I tried my best to be at least as faithful to the needs of my family, especially my spouse, as I have to the demands of my boss? Why or why not? What needs to change?

5. As a community, do our concerns about balancing the parish's finances and beautifying the building and grounds ever distract us from ministering to the spiritual needs of the people who call our parish home?

GOING FORWARD...

One thing I/we can do to help strike a better balance between God and Caesar is...

The first step I/we would need to take is...

CLOSING PRAYER

Lord,
help me to be a
  loyal, compassionate, productive,
    citizen of my country.
Yet may I always remember
  that I am first a citizen
    of the Kingdom of God.

(PARAPHRASING ST. THOMAS MORE)

Is my attitude toward wealth a Christian attitude?

Then he told them a parable: "The land of a rich man produced abundantly. And he thought to himself, 'What should I do, for I have no place to store my crops?' Then he said, 'I will do this: I will pull down my barns and build larger ones, and there I will store all my grain and my goods. And I will say to my soul, Soul, you have ample goods laid up for many years; relax, eat, drink, be merry.' But God said to him, 'You fool! This very night your life is being demanded of you. And the things you have prepared, whose will they be?' So it is with those who store up treasures for themselves but are not rich toward God."

✝ LUKE 12:16–21

He looked up and saw rich people putting their gifts into the treasury; he also saw a poor widow put in two small copper coins. He said, "Truly I tell you, this poor widow has put in more than all of them; for all of them have contributed out of their abundance, but she out of her poverty has put in all she had to live on." ✝ LUKE 21:1–4

11

Taken together, these passages from Luke's gospel present two distinct attitudes toward wealth. There is no question that the rich man in the first story has more than enough to meet his own needs and, presumably, the needs of all who depend upon him. This was true even before his bumper crop. (In a modern context, an equivalent situation would be the year when one's stock portfolio increases well beyond expectation or when one accumulates an extraordinary amount of overtime pay.) What should he do with this unexpected abundance?

His answer is to build even bigger barns—we might think in terms of bigger bank accounts—in which he can store this abundance. Now he will never have to work another day in his life and he can spend the rest of his days in leisure. Ironically, his plan does work out, but not in the way he expected. He will never have to work another day of his life, because this day will be his last.

The widow, on the other hand, finds herself in quite a different situation. She only knows scarcity. Never mind about the uncertainty of her future; there is a real question about whether or not she has enough even for today. Yet when she is given an opportunity to help the poor—think of the Temple treasury as the equivalent of a "poor box" in the back of a church—she holds back nothing. She is not even thinking of her own needs as she throws the only two coins she has to her name into the treasury.

Jesus leaves us with no question as to which of the two he blesses.

What is the fundamental difference between these two people? Why does Jesus bless the one and denounce the other as a fool? Is there something inherently good about poverty and evil about wealth? Not really. Scripture itself proclaims that the *love* of wealth is the root of all evil, not the amount of earthly goods themselves. Certainly, we can consider the example of the wealthy Joseph of

Arimathea who donates his private tomb to Jesus or of the repentant (and likely very rich) tax collectors named Zacchaeus and Levi/ Matthew as evidence that wealth does not have to corrupt. Much more important is the *attitude* one has toward his or her wealth and the relative importance of that wealth in one's life. The rich fool is not foolish because he died that evening—no one knows when mortal life will end. He is a fool because he has allowed his wealth to insulate him from everyone around him. (Notice, in the first story, there is no indication that the rich fool is thinking about anyone but himself.) He has allowed his wealth to replace God as the rock upon which his life is built. Spiritually, it becomes the rock upon which his ship founders.

The widow, however, has no such wealth to separate her from the ever-present needs of the poor. She knows the desperate pain and suffering of poverty. There is nothing good about such poverty in itself, of course—in fact, Jesus and the church exhort us to do all we can to ease the sufferings of the poor. But through her poverty, the widow has come to understand the power of a simple act of generosity. Likely, she has been on the receiving end of more than one such act. (Being a widow in biblical times, when women rarely owned property and did not possess many rights under the law, was an awful place to be. Unless she was young enough and desirable enough to find a second husband, she might very well be faced with the choice of begging or prostitution as the only ways to support herself and her children.) The widow's "rock" is not wealth— it cannot be—but instead is the love of God.

The parable of the rich fool and the story of the poor widow present us with two extremes on a continuum. The rich fool represents absolute trust in material wealth—a dependency that will eventually fail—and by her actions the poor widow seems to be relying solely on God. Her decision is reminiscent of some victims of hurricane Harvey, which devastated the Texas Gulf coast in 2017. News sources were filled with stories and images of brave and generous citizens who, even though they had lost many of their own belongings and, in some cases, their homes were only concerned with helping neighbors worse off than they were to reach higher and safer ground.

Taken together, there is one more important question these two stories implicitly raise. If the economic life of a society results in such overabundant wealth for some and such desperate poverty for others, can we honestly call that society just? Would Jesus? As we approach a disproportionate allocation of wealth in the United States not seen since the 1920s, what must Jesus think about us?

We profess on Sunday and through our prayers that Jesus Christ is the source of our joy and our security, which should put us toward the widow's end of the continuum. Yet if we honestly and comprehensively examine our attitudes toward wealth—as indicated by our actions and not our words—are we in fact closer to the widow, or closer to the fool?

FOR REFLECTION and DISCUSSION

1. Do I see in wealth an opportunity to provide a comfortable life for myself and my family in harmony with the moral teachings of the church? Or do I find at times that I seek a sense of security and well-being from wealth that can only really come from God?

2. When I look at the overall wealth I have accumulated, do I attribute that accumulation only to my own efforts, or do I recognize that I have also benefited from a certain amount of good fortune and the work of others? How does even asking that question make me feel?

3. Do I donate to charity for the sole purpose of helping the poor? Is there a part of my giving that is done with the hope that others notice?

4. When I set up my monthly budget, do I allow a certain percentage for charitable giving? Is it sufficient?

5. On a scale of 1 to 10, with 1 being "not at all" and 10 being "wealth is everything," how would we rate the connection most of us in the parish feel between material wealth and happiness? Why? In which direction does the balance seem to be shifting?

GOING FORWARD...

In the coming weeks, I/we will do the following to increase the amounts of time, talent, and treasure I/we will share with those in need...

The first step in making these changes would be...

CLOSING PRAYER

Holy Spirit,
help us to connect more deeply
with our family and friends,
with our community,
with the neediest among us,
and with our best selves.
Create within us the consistent desire
to place people over profits.
Amen.

Is my attitude toward wealth informed by faith?

He said to his disciples, "Therefore I tell you, do not worry about your life, what you will eat, or about your body, what you will wear. For life is more than food, and the body more than clothing. Consider the ravens: they neither sow nor reap, they have neither storehouse nor barn, and yet God feeds them. Of how much more value are you than the birds! And can any of you by worrying add a single hour to your span of life? If then you are not able to do so small a thing as that, why do you worry about the rest? Consider the lilies, how they grow: they neither toil nor spin; yet I tell you, even Solomon in all his glory was not clothed like one of these. But if God so clothes the grass of the field, which is alive today and tomorrow is thrown into the oven, how much more will he clothe you—you of little faith! And do not keep striving for what you are to eat and what you are to drink, and do not keep worrying. For it is the nations of the world that strive after all these things, and your Father knows that you need them. Instead, strive for his kingdom, and these things will be given to you as well. ✝ LUKE 12:22–31

Sometimes things really do get lost in translation. When viewed in the original Greek, the phrase commonly rendered, "O ye of little faith," literally means, "little faith ones." There is something delightful about that phrasing; it seems more of a term of endearment than a condemnation. Jesus knows so well that, like sheep who quite easily get lost, so many of his beloved children begin to lose their way in fear the moment the next crisis hits. Reminded of our vulnerability and lack of control, we panic. "Where is God?" we cry as we feverishly work on our own personal tower of Babel, using our material wealth in a vain attempt to ward off what we perceive as an onrushing threat. In moments that call for a dollop of faith, we anxiously try to use the material to substitute for the spiritual. As in the Tower of Babel story (see Meditation 20), it is an endeavor doomed to failure.

There is nothing wrong with prudence. In fact, prudence is one of the four cardinal virtues. There are people who depend upon us financially—children, employees, worthy charities, those who benefit from our contributions to federal, state, and local taxes. Life is filled with the unexpected, and it is important to have sufficient savings to handle life's financial necessities and emergencies. Yet once again the implicit question that confronted the rich fool surfaces: How much is enough? In addition to the sin of selfishness illustrated in that earlier parable, Jesus' words in this passage point to a second motivation for hoarding material wealth—a fundamental lack of faith in God. Do we really take Jesus at his word when he tells us that God knows what we need and will provide it? Those of us who have been blessed with a certain amount of material comfort, as we attempt to maintain, manage, and grow our wealth, would do well to take this question into prayer often: Are we acting out of the virtue of prudence, or are we trying to create an impenetrable wall against potential trouble so that faith will not be necessary?

Life can never offer such guarantees. In fact, it is often only in the act of placing our trust in God that real transformation occurs. The point at which we acknowledge that we are not the master builder is the point at which we give God permission to enter into our lives. Some years ago, I saw a poster featuring a cute kitten desperately clinging to the limb of a tree. Underneath the photo was a caption: "Faith isn't faith until there is nothing else to hold onto." That poster captures well the experience of parents or grandparents who, when reflecting upon how they were able to feed, clothe, and educate a large family through difficult financial times, smile at the realization that, somehow, they always "found a way."

Jesus' exhortation in the passage to "consider the lilies" (imagining a field of wildflowers is a better image and closer to Jesus' meaning) reminds us that building an impenetrable wall against disaster is neither possible nor necessary. It also offers us a new lens through which we can more clearly see God's presence—the sacramental nature of creation. I was reminded of this truth so powerfully the other night when I was sitting in my backyard at dusk and saw some sort of an unusual bird—at first, I thought it was a bat—fly down and land on the branch of a nearby tree. I walked over to the tree to get a closer look. When I peered into the two eyes staring back at me I realized to my delight that, for the first time in my life, I was looking at an owl in the wild.

As we take time to appreciate the natural beauty that surrounds us—even in the city we catch a glimpse of God's glory—we are reminded that life has always found a way, even before the creation of 401Ks! True, we are not birds or flowers—but that is precisely Jesus' point. Could the God who provides so abundantly for these creatures ever forget about the needs of God's children?

FOR REFLECTION *and* DISCUSSION

1. Take a few moments to simply observe the natural world around you. Consider these questions: What do I notice? In what ways do I see God's care and concern for creation evident?

2. What is the balance between prayer of petition (asking prayer) and prayer of thanksgiving in my life?

3. After hearing this passage, how do I feel? Imagine yourself in the field with Jesus as he points out the birds and the flowers. Use all of your five senses to place yourself in the scene. What does Jesus have to say to me? What questions arise concerning the idea that "God always provides"?

4. What do I really need? How much of the "stuff" in my life really serves a useful purpose? Keep in mind that leisure time and activity should always be included under the term "useful purpose."

5. How much of the life of our parish faith community is built on faith? How much on fear? Consider this question from a number of angles: Spiritually? Financially? Socially? Emotionally? Intellectually?

GOING FORWARD...

In the week to come, I/we will make the following "leap of faith"...

I/we will demonstrate this leap in the following way(s)...

CLOSING PRAYER

Lord Jesus,
help me to rest in your love.
Remind me that you know my needs
  and the needs of those I love
 much better than I ever can.
May your Spirit guide me
 to seek to love and to be loved
  more than to seek protection.
Amen.

Am I truly generous?

Now the whole group of those who believed were of one heart and soul, and no one claimed private ownership of any possessions, but everything they owned was held in common. With great power the apostles gave their testimony to the resurrection of the Lord Jesus, and great grace was upon them all. There was not a needy person among them, for as many as owned lands or houses sold them and brought the proceeds of what was sold.

But a man named Ananias, with the consent of his wife Sapphira, sold a piece of property; with his wife's knowledge, he kept back some of the proceeds, and brought only a part and laid it at the apostles' feet. "Ananias," Peter asked, "why has Satan filled your heart to lie to the Holy Spirit and to keep back part of the proceeds of the land? While it remained unsold, did it not remain your own? And after it was sold, were not the proceeds at your disposal? How is it that you have contrived this deed in your heart? You did not lie to us but to God!"

✝ ACTS 4:32–34; 5:1–4

~~~~~~~~~

Was the early church a subversive, communist organization? That is the reaction passages such as these sometimes provoke in listeners raised on the milk of capitalism. In truth, the church holds more or less the same view of both ideologies. We who make up the body of Christ recognize that both communism and capitalism are economic systems—means of allocating scarce goods and services to meet unlimited needs and wants—with political implications. Neither one should be confused with the teachings of the church that are worthy of our strict belief and adherence.

Pope St. John Paul II made this point very forcefully and eloquently after the fall of the Berlin Wall and the collapse of the Soviet Union. The pope affirmed that as it was practiced in the Soviet Union, communism was inextricably tied up with totalitarianism and atheism and had justly been tossed into the dustbin of history. He also cautioned, however, against thinking that capitalism had "won." In its insistence that the right to private ownership is unlimited—in other words, that the wealthy have no obligation to share with the poor and to change unjust social structures— capitalism, the pope wrote, contains many elements that are also at odds with Catholic teaching.

A key to making sense of this passage, and to understanding what Pope St. John Paul II was really driving at, is to reflect upon what being generous means when considered from a Christian point of view. As often happens in Scripture, the passage offers us two starkly contrasting examples. The general attitude of the "whole group" was to share everything they owned in common— not because they were required to do so, but because they wanted to do so. Likely their motivation was twofold. By word and example, Jesus had demonstrated time and time again that the only way he could really understand and, ultimately, heal the poor and oppressed among the people of his time was to have a share in their poverty by living and working among them. His disciples, united in "one heart and soul," sought to do the same out of their love for Christ.

Second, the early church included significant membership among the poor—simple laborers, subsistence farmers, and shepherds who generally lived on the precipice of dire poverty. Sharing communal wealth, meager as it might have been, was the best they could do to create a kind of social "safety net" that would catch those in economic and social free fall. At its core, this desire to share everything was rooted in love, and loving actions are always characterized by a certain joy, a certain spontaneity, and a certain abundance. It is significant that none of those in "the whole group" are mentioned by name. Just as St. Francis would have much preferred anonymity, so I imagine did they.

The second part of the reading serves as a contrast to the first. We meet a married couple who are mentioned by name: Ananias and Sapphira. Although they too place a great amount of material wealth at the service of the community—likely much more than most—their motivation is markedly different. Their decision to give only some of their property to the community but say that they have donated all of it suggests that they wish to *appear* to demonstrate the same level of generosity as the rest when they are, in fact, not as generous. By the grace of the Holy Spirit, which is now animating the early Christian community, Peter sees the duplicity and calls them on it: "Why has Satan filled your heart to lie to the Holy Spirit?"

Many who read this second part of the passage will find it troubling. (I have actually edited out the verses that depict their fates.) Regardless of their motivation, shouldn't it matter more *what* they gave than *how* they gave it? Peter's reaction makes it clear that the answer to that question is no. The church can survive on the most meager of material resources (and, in many times and places, has done so and is doing so), but it cannot thrive on meager portions of love. Generosity, in the end, is the tangible evidence of abundant love and compassion. The amount we give is never as important as the spirit in which we give it. "Do small things with great love," as St. Teresa of Calcutta often said.

Shane Claiborne, an evangelical minister deeply involved in social justice work, puts it this way: If we practice the generosity of Jesus, then "capitalism won't be possible and communism won't be necessary."

FOR REFLECTION *and* **DISCUSSION**

1. Have I ever performed an act of charity without seeking something in return?

2. On a scale of 1 to 10, what percentage of my charitable giving is done with an eye to how I am perceived? How much is done out of a spirit of love? How much out of a sense of obligation? A desire for a tax deduction?

3. Have I ever had my generosity ignored or taken for granted? How did that make me feel? Why?

4. What am I holding back that I can give/should give to others? Why?

5. As a parish, have we ever been challenged to share more of our time, talent, and treasure than we thought we could? What was the result?

GOING FORWARD...

One way I will share/we can share my/our resources in a more generous way in the week to come is...

The first thing I/we must do to make this happen is...

CLOSING PRAYER

Holy Spirit,
help me to be as generous
    as I can be.
Fill my heart with the desire
    to freely share my blessings with others.
Amen.

Where is my treasure?

"Do not store up for yourselves treasures on earth, where moth and rust consume and where thieves break in and steal; but store up for yourselves treasures in heaven, where neither moth nor rust consumes and where thieves do not break in and steal. For where your treasure is, there your heart will be also.

"No one can serve two masters; for a slave will either hate the one and love the other, or be devoted to the one and despise the other. You cannot serve God and wealth."

✝ **MATTHEW 6:19–21, 24**

~~~~~~~~~

"Who's your daddy?" This colloquial (and admittedly somewhat sexist!) expression from several decades ago gets to the heart of what Jesus is preaching. From the time we are little, we are taught the First Commandment, which in essence requires us to keep God first in our lives so that we might be in right relationship both with God and with others. There are so many ways the liturgy of the church reminds us of this and calls forth a response from us (for example the *Gloria*, which we pray in Mass, proclaims "Glory to God in the highest and peace to God's people on earth"). The Bible is jam-packed with cautionary tales about what happens to a person, and a community, when this vital commandment is compromised. The story of the golden calf and its consequences in Exodus 32 is a good example.

Yet how deeply has this commandment settled into the inner recesses of our hearts? How often do we pray for guidance before pursuing an opportunity that promises greater wealth and position in one of the earthly hierarchies into which we are all enmeshed? Perhaps we are offered an opportunity to advance in the economic hierarchy by accepting a promotion or a new and more demanding position. Or we get an opportunity to advance in the social hierarchy by accepting a leadership position on the parish council or a membership to an exclusive country club or by holding office in the local PTA. If we do pray, is our prayer perfunctory, or is it rooted in a radical openness to God's will over our own? (While the circumstances surrounding the Garden of Gethsemane seem unique, Jesus' willingness to place God's will first even at the expense of his own life demonstrates in an exceedingly clear way what such radical openness to God looks like and what a struggle it can be.) Simply put, does our treasure consist solely and completely in being a disciple of Jesus, or do we compromise upon our baptismal promises in order to protect and serve an earthly "treasure" we have stashed away in our hearts?

One theme that surfaces again and again for me, is that what we do from Monday to Friday has much more to say about whether or not we are serving God and not wealth than what we do on Sunday. The temptation that besets at least some those who practice their faith by regularly receiving the sacraments is to limit "serving God" to a ceremonial context. If I go to Mass every Sunday, the reasoning goes, and observe the Precepts of the Church, then I must be serving God well. It is an attitude not unlike that of the Pharisees whom Jesus confronts on more than one occasion. His criticism is not that the religious observances are bad—Jesus himself was a devout Jew—but that they were insufficient. "Faith without works is dead," as St. James writes.

Such practices, if separated from a life devoted to God, can become mere observances of the letter of the law but not its spirit—"It is mercy I require, not sacrifice," the prophet Hosea proclaims on God's behalf. Unless we place ourselves at the service of those who need us, beginning with our immediate circle of family and friends but not limited to them, we are not truly serving God. Furthermore, true service to God—and by extension of neighbor—means going beyond meeting whatever needs we can meet today and working with others to make structural changes. We are called to impact society so that needs that arise out of an unjust distribution of goods, services, and power (for example, homelessness) will no longer exist.

Perhaps Jesus' experience in Gethsemane is not so unique. If we are honest with ourselves, we will likely come to the conclusion that the radical commitment to the gospel Jesus calls for in serving God and not wealth could become a threat to our own comfort and well-being. (The book of Job can offer us some insight here. Placed in the mouth of a man who has suffered overwhelming loss, we find both the ideal response to loss: "The Lord giveth and the Lord taketh away, blessed be the name of the Lord" as well as the more human response: "I cry to you and you do not answer me; I stand, and you merely look at me. You have turned cruel to me." Job's struggles are a reminder that the road of discipleship is often shrouded in fog.)

Where is your treasure? Where is your heart's delight stored? It is only when we can say without qualification that the answer to both questions is "with God" that we can truly be free.

FOR REFLECTION *and* DISCUSSION

1. Imagine that you were about to be stranded on a desert island, with no way to call for help, for one year. Answer this question: If I could only take five personal items with me, what would they be? Why?

2. How often do I pray before making an important decision in my life? When I do pray, how much of my prayer is for the ability to accept God's will and how much is an attempt to "sway" God?

3. Reflect upon a time when you spent your energies pursuing a goal that turned out not to be in accord with God's will for your life. Consider these two questions: How did I know? What did I learn from the experience?

4. Complete this statement: *My treasure is...*

5. When were we as a parish led by God along a path that turned out to be the right one for us even though following the path required all of us to make sacrifices? How did we know and what did we learn? What sacrifices might the Spirit be calling upon all of us to make at this time?

GOING FORWARD...

As an individual and as a community, one thing we need to do more of/less of in order to better keep God first is...

If I/we were really doing this, my/our life would change in the following way...

CLOSING PRAYER

Lord Jesus,
we long to serve God.
Too often, however, we serve wealth.
Grant us the grace to discern your call
    from the siren calls of the world.
Transform our hearts
    so that love for you
    transcends all other love.
Amen.

Am I aware
of my abundance?

*As he went ashore, he saw a great crowd; and he had compassion
for them, because they were like sheep without a shepherd; and
he began to teach them many things. When it grew late, his
disciples came to him and said, "This is a deserted place, and
the hour is now very late; send them away so that they may go
into the surrounding country and villages and buy something
for themselves to eat." But he answered them, "You give them
something to eat." They said to him, "Are we to go and buy two
hundred denarii worth of bread, and give it to them to eat?"
And he said to them, "How many loaves have you? Go and see."
When they had found out, they said, "Five, and two fish." Then
he ordered them to get all the people to sit down in groups on the
green grass....Taking the five loaves and the two fish, he looked
up to heaven, and blessed and broke the loaves, and gave them to
his disciples to set before the people; and he divided the two fish
among them all. And all ate and were filled; and they took up
twelve baskets full of broken pieces and of the fish. Those who had
eaten the loaves numbered five thousand men.* ✝ **MARK 6:34–44**

///////////

The story of the multiplication of the loaves and fish is the most widely circulated miracle story in the gospels. With minor variations, the story is repeated six times within the gospels of Mark, Matthew, Luke, and John. The text serves as an invitation to meditation on a variety of themes: the meaning of discipleship, the love of Jesus for all, and the meaning of the Eucharist. What strikes me most powerfully when I consider this story, however, are the baskets of leftovers.

Before Jesus performs the miracle, the story tells us that the disciples had brought a few loaves of bread and a few fish to Jesus. After feeding something like twenty thousand people (the five thousand only includes the men, not the women and children who must also have been present) the disciples collect twelve baskets full of leftovers.

Twelve baskets. That means there were more leftovers at the end of the story than there was food at the beginning!

Had Jesus wished to do so, he certainly could have calculated the caloric intake required by every man, woman, and child in the crowd and brought forth enough food to satisfy each of them down to the last crumb. The obvious abundance of food is so overwhelming that the four gospel writers must certainly have wanted us to notice it. Perhaps, this detail suggests, the belief common to faithful Christians that "God will always give us what we need" is not true. Rather, the grace that God, through the risen Christ, pours into our lives and the blessings we receive is, in fact, far beyond what we need. These abundant blessings are not sufficient; they are ridiculous. There is no way we could possibly ever make use ourselves of all that God gives to us.

What do we make of this? The very thought that God overwhelms us with grace is so counterintuitive to our experience of daily life. More often than not it is scarcity that we are aware of, not abundance. There never seems to be enough time or money to do all that we want to do. The only conclusion that makes sense is that God intended for us to be conduits through which abundance might flow to others. It is in the very act of choosing to share, rather than hoard, that we become aware of just how much we really do have.

This principle of "ridiculous abundance" has important applications. Spiritually, it reminds us that the unique gifts of personality, temperament, and ability God has bestowed on each of us cannot really bear fruit until they are developed through the guidance of the Holy Spirit and shared with others. It is only when we find ourselves in a situation when we are called upon to be patient for the sake of another, for example, that we begin to truly plumb the depths of our reservoirs of patience. Materially, it reminds us that our wealth—which, no matter how we have accumulated it, is also ultimately a gift from God—will do us no good until we share it generously.

The first step in sharing our material wealth more generously is to become more aware that we have an abundance. While it might at first be difficult to accept, the truth is that most of us who enjoy a middle- or upper-middle class lifestyle in the developed world have much more than we need. Just consider the economic boom being experienced by businesses aimed at helping us find the perfect body weight (so many diet and exercise books) or giving us a place to store our excess stuff (so many things) or offering us a bewildering and sometimes morally questionable plethora of entertainment opportunities (so much time on our hands). There is a Catholic social justice principle, ancient in its origins but emphasized by Pope St. John Paul II, Pope Benedict XVI, and Pope Francis, that is especially relevant in the modern world. It states that all of us have an obligation to give our surplus to the poor—not out of charity, but out of justice.

As I reflect upon my own financial situation through the years, for example, something always strikes me as odd. When my wife and I had just purchased our home and were both settling in and preparing for the birth of our first child, we had virtually no savings and ever mounting expenses. Yet despite my occasional bouts of financial anxiety, I experienced an abiding sense that, somehow, God would provide. Now that we are older and have accumulated at least a modest nest egg to provide for future expenses, I find myself continually checking my IRA. It seems at times that the more we accumulate, the less secure I feel! Yet the truth is quite the opposite.

There is nothing wrong—and much that is good—about wanting to use our wealth in such a way as to help provide a comfortable and wholesome life for our families and ourselves. There is something wrong, however, about an attitude of entitlement and ingratitude. The more we are aware of our wealth as an abundance and as a gift from God, the more we will be willing to share it with those in need.

FOR REFLECTION *and* **DISCUSSION**

1. What are the blessings of abundance in my life that I am aware of at this time? How specifically and completely can I name them?

2. When I say to myself that "God will provide," what particular situations and memories in my life come to mind? How, specifically, have I seen the truth of this in my life?

3. If I really believed that my family's well-being had more to do with relying on God than relying on my own efforts, how would my priorities shift? How much of the energy that I spend on making a living and saving for the future is motivated by fear or greed?

4. Imagine that you are among the crowd that has been fed to bursting by Jesus. Imagine further that Jesus walks among the crowds until he sits down next to you. Consider these two questions: What do I have to say to Jesus? What does Jesus have to say to me?

5. What is the level of entitlement experienced by people of my generation? Do we seem in general to be appreciative of all that God has blessed us with? (Please note: It is very important that you focus as much as you possibly can only on yourself and your peers and avoid the cynical and almost always false "things were better in the old days/the next generation is going to hell in a hand basket" temptation.)

GOING FORWARD...

This week, I/ we will remind ourselves of the abundance that Jesus has provided me/us individually and as a community by...

One action that would demonstrate a change in my/our attitude would be...

CLOSING PRAYER

Lord Jesus,
thank you for all of the blessings in our lives;
    especially, I am grateful for _____ .
      (Allow each person in the group to offer a specific blessing.)
Send the Holy Spirit
    to create in each of one of us
    a heart that is more generous
      and more grateful
      and more able to be a conduit
    of your grace to others.
Amen.

Who am I stepping over?

"There was a rich man who was dressed in purple and fine linen and who feasted sumptuously every day. And at his gate lay a poor man named Lazarus, covered with sores, who longed to satisfy his hunger with what fell from the rich man's table; even the dogs would come and lick his sores. The poor man died and was carried away by the angels to be with Abraham. The rich man also died and was buried. In Hades, where he was being tormented, he looked up and saw Abraham far away with Lazarus by his side. He called out, 'Father Abraham, have mercy on me, and send Lazarus to dip the tip of his finger in water and cool my tongue; for I am in agony in these flames.' But Abraham said, 'Child, remember that during your lifetime you received your good things, and Lazarus in like manner evil things; but now he is comforted here, and you are in agony. Besides all this, between you and us a great chasm has been fixed, so that those who might want to pass from here to you cannot do so, and no one can cross from there to us.' He said, 'Then, father, I beg you to send him to my father's house—for I have five brothers—that he may warn them, so that they will not also come into this place of torment.' Abraham replied, 'They have Moses and the prophets; they should listen to them.' He said, 'No, father Abraham; but if someone goes to them from the dead, they will repent.' He said

to him, 'If they do not listen to Moses and the prophets, neither will they be convinced even if someone rises from the dead.'"
✛ LUKE 16:19–31

⁓⁓⁓⁓⁓⁓⁓⁓

The full impact of this story did not hit me until my wife and I took a vacation that included an afternoon at the ruins of Pompeii. Walking through the streets of this ancient Roman town, preserved by the collapsed ash cloud caused by the eruption of Mt. Vesuvius in 79 AD, is like walking almost two thousand years back in time. All of the wooden roofs of the buildings are gone, but the first-floor shops, houses, and streets look pretty much as they did the day the volcano erupted. When you walk through the massive gateway leading into the city, you feel that time travel is really possible.

As we followed our guide along the designated tourist route, he stopped at one point in front of a nondescript doorway leading into a private dwelling. He explained to us that life in ancient cities was cramped. The defensive walls that surrounded the town made expansion difficult; thus, every available square foot within the walls had to be used efficiently. From the street, a rich man's house such as the one we were standing in front of looked no different than any other dwelling. When you walked inside the house, however, the contrast was stark; a number of rooms were linked in the form of a rectangle surrounding a garden filled with flowers and fountains. Given the mild Mediterranean climate, these rooms could be left open to the fresh air in the courtyard, creating a personal oasis for the family. All that was visible to the general public, however, was that simple doorway. I have often wondered: When Jesus said that the poor Lazarus was "lying at the rich man's door," was this the kind of door he had in mind? Certainly there must have been similar houses in the Roman towns of Galilee with which Jesus would have been familiar—specifically, the cities of Tiberius and Sephoris.

Once I made this connection, the story really began to speak to me. The rich man would literally have had to step over poor Lazarus each and every time he entered and exited his home. And not once did he even notice that Lazarus was there. Even the dogs who, by licking his sores might have provided a bit of comfort to Lazarus, paid more attention to him.

The rich man's final destiny in that place of eternal torment was not due to anything he had done wrong. Nowhere in the story does Jesus indicate that the rich man ever harassed, mocked, or abused Lazarus. There is no indication that Lazarus' plight was directly caused by the rich man. It seems that the sin of the rich man was a sin of omission—his relationship with God, as it was with Lazarus, was broken by what he did *not* do.

Who are the people we step over? The "invisible people" that we have stopped noticing—if we ever did in the first place? This is a question to reflect upon on a number of levels. Certainly, we can begin on the personal level. Is there someone in my life whom I am taking for granted or whom I have pigeonholed or stereotyped so that I do not really have to interact with him/her? Is there someone that, for whatever reason, I have come to believe or have been conditioned to believe that I can treat badly? Seeking answers to such questions within the depth of our consciences will be hard work, but good people are at least willing to make the attempt.

The question may become much more challenging, however, when we apply it to issues of stewardship and wealth. For example, when I find that great bargain on an item of clothing, have

I ever stopped to ask *why* it is so cheap? Who has made the sacrifice—perhaps against his or her will—of their time, labor, and economic opportunity so that I could benefit? How much of the price I pay for manufactured goods is subsidized by the unreasonably low wages and long hours endured by a factory worker somewhere in the world? When I find that low-price hotel room that allows me to enjoy an affordable vacation with my family and friends, have I ever wondered if part of that discount is at the expense of the low-wage workers who clean my room and perform any number of menial tasks in the complex? The world is simply filled with "invisible people" who fill the minimum wage jobs of the world.

These are much harder reflections to undertake. Given how hard we work for our money, we may even resent having to look at the questions at all. Yet whether we choose to really see Lazarus in our world, he is there, lying at our doorsteps. How can we honor them and help them now, so that we might join them in the bosom of Abraham later?

FOR REFLECTION *and* **DISCUSSION**

1. Where do I see Lazarus in my life? In my community? In my parish? In my city and state?

2. Do I really want to Jesus to show me the "invisible people" around me? Why or why not?

3. How would my life have to change if Lazarus came out of the shadows and showed himself to me? What would be the hardest part of my lifestyle to change? Why?

4. What are my feelings toward Lazarus and the rich man? With whom do I sympathize? Why?

5. What are some things our parish is doing, or can do, to find and to reach out to the "invisible people" around us?

GOING FORWARD...

One specific change in my life I/we can make right now which would make it more likely I/we will notice Lazarus is...

One thing I/we can do that will contribute to structural change so that less people will find themselves in Lazarus' position is...

Our parish can contribute to this change by doing...

CLOSING PRAYER

Holy Spirit,
open my eyes,
*   open my heart,*
guide my steps,
so that I always
*   walk in solidarity*
*   with my sister and with my brother.*
Amen.

Is my wealth too "sticky"?

Then someone came to him and said, "Teacher, what good deed must I do to have eternal life?" And he said to him, "Why do you ask me about what is good? There is only one who is good. If you wish to enter into life, keep the commandments." He said to him, "Which ones?" And Jesus said, "You shall not murder; You shall not commit adultery; You shall not steal; You shall not bear false witness; Honor your father and mother; also, You shall love your neighbor as yourself." The young man said to him, "I have kept all these; what do I still lack?" Jesus said to him, "If you wish to be perfect, go, sell your possessions, and give the money to the poor, and you will have treasure in heaven; then come, follow me." When the young man heard this word, he went away grieving, for he had many possessions.

Then Jesus said to his disciples…. "I tell you, it is easier for a camel to go through the eye of a needle than for someone who is rich to enter the kingdom of God." ✛ MATTHEW 19:16–24

~~~~~~~~~

The ways that we can become overly attached to our wealth are subtle, but real. Time and time again in the Scriptures, often through metaphors, Jesus warns us about these traps. It isn't wealth itself that is inherently evil. As it is written in 1 Timothy 6:10, "the *love* of money is the root of all evil." Material wealth can be used to do much good. A careful reading of the gospels as well as Acts of the Apostles will reveal that there were a number of women and men of means who supported Jesus' ministry and showed great generosity in their material support of the early church. This continues to be true in modern times, as illustrated for example by the life of Saint Elizabeth Seton, a widow who used her wealth after her husband died to found a school for Christian education and the Sisters of Charity. Certainly, all of us have examples in our own lives of acts of financial generosity that benefited a worthy cause.

What the story of the meeting between Jesus and the rich young man points out is that wealth is not "inert." If we are not vigilant, attachments grow very subtly and easily, connecting our wealth and our sense of well-being. How easily we can begin to believe that our future happiness is dependent on that wealth and not on God. Gradually, almost without us perceiving it, that place at the core of each one of our lives reserved for the risen Christ begins to fill with something else.

The story makes it clear that there is no question about the young man's desire to live a good life. He sought out Jesus to ask the most important question any one of us can ask of God: "What must I do to inherit eternal life?" He affirms in the presence of Jesus that he is faithfully doing his best to keep the commandments. Yet, clearly, something big is missing. He is in essence asking Jesus to fill the emptiness inside of him.

Jesus, the good and loving physician, diagnoses the problem. "Sell your possessions…give the money to the poor…then come, follow me," he says. Just as a diet of junk food might fill the stomach but will never satisfy our nutritional needs, the young man's dependence on material wealth will never satisfy his spiritual needs. In order for Jesus to fill up that space at the center of his soul, the "material junk food" has to go. We can only pray and hope that the realization Jesus gifts him with on this day (which makes him sad for the moment) on another day became the source of his joy.

Jesus' concluding reflection drives the point home: "It is easier for a camel to pass through the eye of a needle than for a rich man to get into heaven." Through the use of hyperbole, an exaggeration intended to grab our attention and get us thinking, the good teacher makes it clear that the young man's situation is not an isolated example. Without sufficient prayer and vigilance, the wealth that we possess can begin to possess us.

FOR REFLECTION *and* DISCUSSION

1. Imagine Jesus is asking you the question, "What do you lack?" How do you answer?

2. In what way in my life at this moment is Jesus asking me to "sell all you have and follow me"? (Be as specific as you can.)

3. Imagine the next few weeks in the life of the rich young man. Will he change? How?

4. What would be the hardest thing for me to give up if Jesus asked me to do so? Why?

5. As a parish, what do we seek from Jesus at this time? What do we need in order to embrace our call more fully to be a Christian community?

GOING FORWARD...

One thing I/we can do to create more space in the center of my/our lives for Christ in the coming week is...

CLOSING PRAYER

Lord Jesus,
send your Spirit
    into the very marrow of my being.
May the Spirit's wind and fire
    clear out all that I depend on that is not YOU
so that you might fill that space
    with your peace,
    with your love,
        and with your Presence.
Amen.

Am I losing my sense of solidarity with the poor?

Hear this, you that trample on the needy,
    and bring to ruin the poor of the land,
saying, "When will the new moon be over
    so that we may sell grain;
and the sabbath,
    so that we may offer wheat for sale?
We will make the ephah small and
    the shekel great,
    and practice deceit with false balances,
Buying the poor for silver
    and the needy for a pair of sandals,
    and selling the sweepings of the wheat."
The Lord has sworn by the pride of Jacob:
Surely I will never forget any of their deeds.

✝ AMOS 8:4–7

~~~~~~~~~

At first some of the language may be obscure, but with a little con-
textual background, God's condemnation of the rich as conveyed

by the prophet Amos becomes crystal clear. How do the rich "trample on the needy"? Not through obvious acts of thievery. The genius in the exploitation of the poor by the wealthy in Amos' society is its subtlety. Unless one looks closely (the way that God looks) the poor man or woman might not even realize it is happening.

An "ephah" is a unit of measurement of dry goods, particularly produce, that is something like a bushel. To "make the ephah small and the shekel [the standard coin of the ancient Jewish realm] great" is to overcharge. The poor, forced to buy food to supplement the meager crops they were growing (much of which was likely given to the landowner as payment) are further preyed upon by the merchant who is fixing his scales. The difference is so small that it is difficult to prove. Over time, however, the cheating adds up to significant sums.

While literally "buying the poor for silver" in the form of slavery is forbidden in the Jewish Torah, the poor who had gone into debt for the reasons cited above would be forced to borrow money at exorbitant interest rates. Legally, the poor subsistence farmer (who is in debt to the rich man for the foreseeable future) might be free, but his ability to take control of his own life is severely compromised. As illustrated by exception in Jesus' parable about the wealthy man who forgives his servant's debt, the poor would likely spend years in the service of the wealthy working off what they owed.

Probably as a result of these harsh conditions, a custom developed. It provided at least a minimal amount of help to the poor in a society that lacked any kind of social safety net. When the time for the wheat harvest came, the landowner was supposed to leave the grain growing around the edges of the field untouched. These remnants of the crop would then be available to anyone who was hungry and who might be walking along one of the roads that ran along the field's edges. Yet even that small act of charity was too much of a sacrifice for at least some of the rich in Amos' day who are determined to sell even the "sweepings of the wheat."

How does such a callous disregard for the needs of others take root in a society and in the hearts of some of its members? Certainly, things didn't start out that way. The kingdom of Israel within which Amos lived and prophesied was only a few centuries removed from the humble beginnings of the freed Hebrew slaves who settled in the Promised Land. They had once had a palpable sense of what it was like to be poor and oppressed. (Not much further from this beginning, relatively speaking, than the United States is from its colonial origins.)

So how did the callous disregard take root? Gradually. Ambition gave way to arrogance, reverence to comfort, industry to greed. Again, the "stickiness" of wealth shows itself. Wealth insulates. As a recognition of God's special care and concern for the poor is lost, it becomes much easier to exploit them. It is hard to say when this society lost its moral way, but Amos proclaims with divine certainty that it had.

Somewhere along the line, the rich lost touch with God. Sabbaths and sacred feasts became meaningless rituals to be hurried through ("When will the new moon be over so that we can sell our grain?") so that further business could be conducted. And with a loss of solidarity with God comes a loss of solidarity with other people—a solidarity characterized by a powerful recognition that the welfare of strangers, most especially if they are poor or oppressed, matters to all of us. It's hard to say which was lost first—the connection with God or with those in need. In the end, it doesn't really matter, because the loss of one inevitably leads to the loss of the other.

If we who live in one of the wealthiest countries in the world find parallels to the conditions and attitudes Amos describes in our own society, it would be wise for us to take notice.

FOR REFLECTION *and* DISCUSSION

1. Have I ever cheated anyone in my business dealings? Have I ever witnessed cheating and remained silent? Have I ever taken for myself or my family a privilege to which I was not entitled? (For example, trying to use a PBA card to get out of a traffic ticket.)

2. In how many of the opportunities to care for the poor offered in my workplace or parish do I take participate? Where do I feel particularly drawn to help?

3. What percentage of my time and income do I give to worthy causes? Have those resources decreased, increased, or stayed the same over the years? Am I in a situation now where I am able to do more?

4. Do I engage in any business practices or am I aware of supporting any businesses that exploit their workers or take advantage of their customers? Am I willing to spend a little more for a product if it comes with assurances that the company has agreed to abide by agreements designed to protect workers from exploitation (an example would be only purchasing coffee with a "Fair Trade" logo)?

5. Is there a ministry aimed at helping the poor that our parish used to support but no longer does? If so, why? What are some new ways our parish might "hear the cry of the poor" at this time, as Jesus always does?

GOING FORWARD...

In the coming weeks, one way I/we will strive to raise my/our conscience and the consciences of others toward the plight of the poor is to...

The first step I/we need to take toward that goal is...

CLOSING PRAYER

Loving Father and Mother,
I know you hear the cry of the poor.
I ask your forgiveness
    for those times
    when I have closed my eyes, ears, and heart
        to the needs of the poor.
Create in me a clean heart,
        new ears, and new eyes
    so that I might see the needs before me
    and be filled with a spirit of compassion.
Amen.

Am I a sheep or a goat?

"When the Son of Man comes in his glory, and all the angels with him, then he will sit on the throne of his glory. All the nations will be gathered before him, and he will separate people one from another as a shepherd separates the sheep from the goats, and he will put the sheep at his right hand and the goats at the left. Then the king will say to those at his right hand, 'Come, you that are blessed by my Father, inherit the kingdom prepared for you from the foundation of the world; for I was hungry and you gave me food, I was thirsty and you gave me something to drink, I was a stranger and you welcomed me, I was naked and you gave me clothing, I was sick and you took care of me, I was in prison and you visited me.' Then the righteous will answer him, 'Lord, when was it that we saw you hungry and gave you food, or thirsty and gave you something to drink? And when was it that we saw you a stranger and welcomed you, or naked and gave you clothing? And when was it that we saw you sick or in prison and visited you?' And the king will answer them, 'Truly I tell you, just as you did it to one of the least of these who are members of my family, you did it to me.'" ✛ MATTHEW 25:31–45

What is most surprising about this parable is what God is *not* interested in come Judgment Day. The criteria used to separate the sheep (the righteous) from the goats (the unrighteous) have nothing (directly) to do with pious practices, net worth, number of children and grandchildren one has produced, or the status one has achieved in the world. There are no questions to test one's theological understanding of mysteries of the faith or dogmas like the Trinity; no subpoenas for financial records indicating how large one's donations were to charity. Fashion sense, the size of one's car, house, or bank account all fall by the wayside. The Son of Man has only one question: What did you do—or not do—for the least of my sisters and brothers?

This story is rooted deeply in our Catholic consciousness. It is the basis for the seven corporal works of mercy, which form an essential part of Catholic moral teaching. But do we really understand how central the corporal works of mercy are? And why they are so central?

The Old Testament prophets proclaim often that "the Lord hears the cry of the poor." Nowhere is this connection between the poor and God made more explicitly clear than in this parable. Each and every time we care for someone in need we are caring for Jesus. And each and every time we turn our backs on someone in need we turn our backs on Christ. The identification is total and airtight. (As I sit here and think about the homeless people I pass by on my commute to work every day, almost without noticing, how I wish this were not so!)

What makes this parable so challenging is not the message, but the intensity of the message. Most of us try to do what we can to help the poor, in some cases making significant sacrifices of time, talent, and treasure in the process. That is the essence of charity, and it has worth. However, what this parable is demanding of us, as we stand face to face with Jesus in the face of the poor, is something much more challenging. If Jesus is as closely identified with the poor and oppressed as he proclaims in this parable, then what we do for those in need constitutes a primary means of worship and prayer. Caring for the poor and oppressed, therefore, is not just a nice thing to do. It is an obligation placed upon us by our baptism.

Precisely because this message is so challenging, we may find ourselves almost subconsciously throwing up intricately constructed rationalizations designed to blunt its force. We may say that the poor are just lazy or that they are gaming the system, even though more sober reflection would make it clear to us that our judgments about the poor are mostly based on opinion and prejudice and that most of the "gaming" that goes on in the world is done by the rich, who have the power to alter the rules of the game to suit them.

Furthermore, we all fall victim to the human failing of "out of sight, out of mind." (Perhaps there is an insight into the meaning of Original Sin here. While most of us are capable of demonstrating great compassion for those in our family and our communities in need, the further removed from us the person or group in need is, the less we tend to notice. One of the effects of Original Sin is a sense that we are somehow separate from one another—that the pain of the person suffering from the famine in East Africa, for example, is not my pain.) The places of pain and suffering Jesus outlines in the parable—places of malnourishment or hunger; places of enforced isolation, such as prisons or hospitals; places of sickness or extreme poverty; places of the dying and the dead, such as war zones—are places most of us do whatever we can to avoid. Unless we have a personal connection with someone in one of these situations, it is easy enough to tuck our concerns into a small corner of our consciousness and go about our business.

We who are true disciples of Christ are good people who sincerely want to bring the message of Jesus' unconditional love to others. We are not wolves in sheep's clothing. However, as we honestly examine the amount of our time and energy and resources we expend to protect ourselves and our families from encountering those places of suffering and the people in them, can we also say that we are never *goats* in sheep's clothing?

FOR REFLECTION *and* **DISCUSSION**

1. How often do I pray for those on the margins of society—the homeless, the poor, the imprisoned, the shut-ins, for example? When something happens that forces me to think of them for a moment (e.g., I encounter a homeless person on the street), what is my first thought and feeling? Am I compassionate or angry?

2. How much of my time, talent, and treasure do I commit to the needs of others in the form of tithing? 10%? 5%? 1%? Less? Has the percentage changed over the years? Why or why not?

3. Who were the people in need that Jesus placed in my path this week? Was my response more like the sheep in the parable or more like the goats?

4. Have I ever personally experienced one of the needs that Jesus describes in the parable? Has anyone I know experienced those needs? What was that experience like?

5. Using the criteria for judgment outlined in this parable, is our parish more "sheeplike" or "goatlike"? Where are we doing a good job in caring for the "least of Jesus' sisters and brothers"? Where are our efforts coming up short?

GOING FORWARD...

One way I/we could become more "sheeplike" and less "goatlike" would be to...

The first step in making this change would be...

CLOSING PRAYER

Lord Jesus,
help us to look beyond
 our fears,
 our greed,
  and our prejudices.
Help us to see you more clearly
 in the face of everyone we meet,
 especially those in need.
Fill our hearts
 with your abundant compassion.
Amen.

Am I with Mary and the poor?

And Mary said,
"My soul magnifies the Lord,
    and my spirit rejoices in God my Savior,
for he has looked with favor on the
      lowliness of his servant.
    Surely, from now on all generations
      will call me blessed;
for the Mighty One has done great things
      for me,
    and holy is his name.
His mercy is for those who fear him
    from generation to generation.
He has shown strength with his arm;
    he has scattered the proud in the thoughts
      of their hearts.
He has brought down the powerful
      from their thrones,
    and lifted up the lowly;
he has filled the hungry with good things,
    and sent the rich away empty.

He has helped his servant Israel,
    in remembrance of his mercy,
according to the promise he made to
        our ancestors,
    to Abraham and to his descendants for ever."

✛ LUKE 1:46–55

~~~~~~~~

Mary's prayer of praise, inspired by her visit with her cousin Elizabeth in Luke's gospel, is one of the most revered passages in the Scriptures. Known by the first word of the prayer in Latin, *Magnificat*, it is an essential part of the Liturgy of the Hours. Familiarity and repetition, however, can sometimes cause us to overlook the implications of what Mary is saying.

Though she is the Mother of God, in this passage Mary unambiguously places herself in solidarity with the poor and marginalized. Mary rejoices because God has looked with favor on her "lowliness" and reflects upon how this is God's consistent pattern. Time and time again, Mary joyously proclaims, God has "brought down the powerful" but "lifted up the lowly." The rich pray to God from a sense of entitlement and are sent away "empty." The hungry, however, realize their dependence on God and so can be "filled with good things." In her joyous proclamation of the wondrous reversals that God initiates in order to overturn the expected way of the world, Mary echoes the teachings of the Hebrew prophets such as Isaiah, who proclaim that the Lord hears the cry of the poor. She anticipates the teaching of Jesus during his adult ministry when he completely identifies God with the poor and lowly with the words, "Whatsoever you do to the least of my sisters and brothers, you do to me."

Such considerations of how closely God identifies with the poor should cause those who have been blessed with a certain amount of wealth and influence to pause and reflect. Are we as attentive to their cry as Mary—and God—always are? Have we emptied ourselves sufficiently of all those things—material and otherwise—which might prevent us from receiving all of the gifts and blessings that God would like to send us? Or are we more like the person featured in the pop song "Pleasant Valley Sunday" who laments: "Creature comfort goals, they only numb my soul/ And make it hard for me to see"?

The Catholic social justice principle of solidarity can help us here. Simply put, this principle states that when Jesus says that all human beings are sisters and brothers, he is not speaking metaphorically. We are one family and therefore responsible for one another. Just as we rejoice when someone we love personally is relieved of his or her suffering, so should we rejoice when we are able to cooperate with God in lifting up those whom society has trodden down. This is the essence of the joy that Mary expresses in the *Magnificat*.

The reason that the rich get sent away empty by God is not because God hates rich people. God loves all of us. I've come to believe that the rich whom Mary refers to in her prayer of praise are sent away empty because there is simply no way that God can satisfy them. The more they accumulate, the more they want. Like the rich fool, they cannot hear the cry of the poor because the whine of their own wants is always in their ears.

Mary, loving mother of Jesus and of the church, can show us a better way. We only need to stand with her, and with all those who may have been overlooked by the world but are never overlooked by God.

FOR REFLECTION *and* DISCUSSION

1. When I ask Mary to help me identify those who need my help at this time, to whom does she direct me?

2. Has there been a "want" I have mistaken for a "need" lately? What is it?

3. Where is solidarity most seriously under attack in our world, our nation, and in my community or workplace at this time? What can I do to be a force of healing and Justice?

4. Is there a privileged position I enjoy that in some way makes it difficult for me to hear and respond to the common good?

5. How can we as a parish use our wealth and resources to lift up the poor and lowly?

GOING FORWARD...

During the coming weeks, when I/we come across someone in need or who is marginalized, I/we will ask: "How would I respond if this person were a member of my family?"

I/we will take the question to prayer, and act upon the answer.

CLOSING PRAYER

Blessed Mother,
you comfort and enfold the church
    with your maternal care.
As you once did at Cana,
    you continue to notice the needs that others miss.
Touch my heart with your gentle love.
Pray for us,
    that we might be more attentive
    to the needs of those
        God has placed in our paths.
Amen.

Is my concern for the poor real or reality TV?

Six days before the Passover Jesus came to Bethany, the home of Lazarus, whom he had raised from the dead. There they gave a dinner for him. Martha served, and Lazarus was one of those at the table with him. Mary took a pound of costly perfume made of pure nard, anointed Jesus' feet, and wiped them with her hair. The house was filled with the fragrance of the perfume. But Judas Iscariot, one of his disciples (the one who was about to betray him), said, "Why was this perfume not sold for three hundred denarii and the money given to the poor?" (He said this not because he cared about the poor, but because he was a thief; he kept the common purse and used to steal what was put into it.) Jesus said, "Leave her alone. She bought it so that she might keep it for the day of my burial. You always have the poor with you, but you do not always have me." + JOHN 12:1–8

Starting with the first season of the television show *Survivor* a number of years ago, the broadcast and cable networks intro-duced us to a novel kind of program: reality TV. Rather than scripted dramas or comedies with professional actors, networks began to experiment with something completely new. Real people were placed in unusual situations designed to create tension, suspense, and drama as they interacted with one another and with the camera. Careful editing and a photogenic commentator acting as the host of the show completed the desired effect. From the point of view of those who created the programs, the cost savings were phenomenal. Rather than shell out millions for an established star, the networks could recruit a host of colorful characters willing to work for nothing but the promise of public recognition and, perhaps, a cash prize.

The catch, of course, is that "reality" television isn't real at all. Hundreds of hours of footage are carefully edited to create whatever storyline the director has in mind. We don't meet the people in the show as they are; rather, we are shown the bits and pieces of film those who produce the show want us to see as they craft both characters and caricatures from the raw material of the on-camera interviews and hidden-camera footage. Reality television is actually a unique type of fiction.

In this Scripture passage, as John tells the story, Judas emerges as a perfect reality TV star. He plays the role of a person deeply committed to the needs of the poor so perfectly. Every action is carefully scripted. What a wasteful use of expensive perfume, he says, dramatically feigning indignity for all to see. Just think how much good that money could have done, he laments, if Mary had not been so foolish and impulsive. (In an aside, John reveals Judas' true motives.) Having played the part of the champion of the poor with a studied perfection, Judas may well have convinced many at that dinner that it was he, not Jesus, who was the real star of the show.

It will not be long, of course, before Judas will reveal himself for the traitor he is. In this story, John gives us a glimpse into the darkness of his heart. Judas pretends to care for the poor when in fact his motives likely are a combination of greed and a desire to discredit Jesus. At the same moment that Mary's action honors Jesus, Judas' words dishonor him.

Before we dismiss Judas as a reality TV star gone bad, however, we might want to take a moment and consider this story as a cautionary tale.

We are Christians, and we know that a willingness to be generous is an essential part of our lives as Jesus' disciples. Certainly, we hear the message preached from the pulpit often enough. Yet when it comes to actually making sacrifices on behalf of those in need, do we sometimes find ourselves content with simply looking the part as Judas did?

I once went on a retreat where the speaker described the two "feet" of social justice. Charity, he said, refers to those voluntary acts of generosity that we perform—donations of time, talent, and treasure—that we do not have to do but which we engage in willingly for the sake of the less fortunate. These actions are good and holy and necessary. And yet there is a whiff of reality TV about them. If we take a moment to reflect upon our own good deeds, especially the kind things that people say about us for doing them or the good feeling we get from performing them—is it not true that at least a small portion of our motivation for such work is the desire to be liked and admired?

Such reflections bring us to the second "foot"—right into the heart of what justice means. Unlike charity, justice is never optional. To seek justice is to recognize that 1) patterns of injustice are deeply woven into our society and 2) people do not benefit from them equally. If we have benefited from them, then we have an obligation to do what we can to change them. To paraphrase Dorothy Day, justice is not about feeding the poor but about asking why they are poor.

Recognizing injustice and working to change structures is not likely to bring us the admiration of others and a warm fuzzy feeling of contentment in the short term. We may not be perceived as champions of goodness. In fact, we might be viewed with suspicion and scorn. If so, we find ourselves in the company of such wise souls as Dr. Martin Luther King Jr., Dorothy Day, and Mahatma Gandhi, whose commitment to justice and not just charity took years to bear fruit. As Jesus proclaims in the Beatitudes, if we incorporate the values of the Kingdom into our lives now—particularly, a "hunger and thirst" for justice—we will find ourselves receiving a final blessing not of our own choosing: "Blessed are you when people insult you and persecute you and falsely say all kinds of evil against you because of me."

It doesn't get any more real than that.

FOR REFLECTION *and* DISCUSSION

1. As I allocate my time, talent, and treasure each week, how much is dedicated to relieving the burdens of others?

2. Am I content with being thought generous? If my acts of generosity were never noticed by anyone, how would I feel? Think deeply about this question.

3. Am I more concerned with what Jesus thinks of me or what other people think of me?

4. In what ways have I benefited from injustice?

5. When we consider our commitment to those in need as a parish, what is the balance between our involvement in charitable giving and our work for justice? Is the balance a good one? Why or why not? How might the risen Christ be challenging us at this time to leave our comfort zone and to work more directly to fix the injustice we see?

GOING FORWARD...

During this coming week I/we will make the following "secret sacrifice" on behalf of someone in need or some important cause...

CLOSING PRAYER

Loving Father and Mother,
there is no heart
   into which you do not see.
There is no secret
   that will not one day be revealed.
Each day,
   under the gentle touch of your hand,
may I become more generous,
   more aware of the injustice around me,
   more committed to making changes,
that will transform the world
    and myself
   into more and more genuine
   reflections of your presence and love.
Amen.

If given the choice, "your money or your life," which would I choose?

Do not desire the ruler's delicacies,
*   for they are deceptive food.*
Do not wear yourself out to get rich;
*   be wise enough to desist.*
When your eyes light upon it, it is gone;
*   for suddenly it takes wings to itself,*
*   flying like an eagle toward heaven.*

+ **PROVERBS 23:3–5**

Jack Benny was a comedian in the middle of the twentieth century. Though he is remembered as being a generous man, much of his comedy was rooted in the running gag that he was very stingy with his money. In one classic sketch, a mugger approaches Benny, gun drawn, and says, "Your money or your life!" A pause ensues. "Well?" the would-be thief demands. "I'm thinking!" Benny replies.

What makes for entertaining comedy turns to tragedy if we get this balance wrong in our lives. Material wealth is "deceptive food" indeed. How much is enough? At what point do we find we have accumulated sufficient wealth so that our fears about future security disappear? That we have fully satiated our desire to accumulate more? Is there such a point, or does it seem that the more we accumulate, the faster that sense of security and well-being "takes wings to itself" and we find ourselves feeling even more insecure and dissatisfied?

Of course, we know that our lives are more valuable than any amount of material wealth, and to think otherwise would be absurd. It is just that recognition that makes Jack Benny's reaction—accentuated by the emphasis with which he delivers it—so funny. Yet if we take an honest look at our list of priorities each day, we may discover a truth that is not so funny. Are we, in fact, "wearing ourselves out" to provide for what we think is necessary to support our family and ourselves? How often do we stop and pray, seeking the wisdom of the Spirit so that we might understand if we have our priorities straight? When our earthly lives come to a close, how will we feel about the hours and the energy we have devoted to securing our economic livelihood? If we really believed that God knows what we need before we do, how would our priorities shift?

Certainly not one of us is so foolish as to choose our wallets over our well-being if forced to make the choice Jack Benny depicts. Yet over the course of our lives, in the face of that persistent, gnawing fear of not having enough and, perhaps, a dash of greed and overarching ambition, it is possible to make the same sad choice. When we sacrifice opportunities to be with our families and our friends, to take advantage of wholesome recreation and rest, to seek a deeper relationship with God, and to work with others to make the world a better place—all in the pursuit of material wealth—we may find out one day that we have never lived at all. And that is nothing to laugh at.

FOR REFLECTION *and* DISCUSSION

1. If I only had twenty-four hours to live, how would I spend that time?

2. It has been said that no one ever dies wishing he or she had spent more time at the office. How do I feel about this statement?

3. As I look back over my life, am I aware of any moments when I had an opportunity to choose between time spent with those people in my life who are important to me and time at the office and chose to work? Do I regret any of these choices? Why?

4. What changes can I make to avoid such pitfalls in the future?

5. If as a parish community we truly believed that God knows our needs better than we do, how would our priorities shift? What ministries would receive more attention? How would we reallocate our resources?

GOING FORWARD...

During this next week I/we will show our faith that God truly does provide for us by the following actions...

One thing I/we can certainly let go of is...

CLOSING PRAYER

Heavenly Father and Mother,
I know that you desire
   only what is good for me,
and that you know what I need
   even before I do.
Teach me to trust.
Send your Holy Spirit
   to burn away
      everything
   that prevents me from having faith
   and that keeps me
      weighed down
   by unholy spirits of selfish desire and fear.
Amen.

How aware am I of the existence of Structural Sin?

The LORD spoke to Moses on Mount Sinai, saying: You shall count off seven weeks of years, seven times seven years, so that the period of seven weeks of years gives forty-nine years. Then you shall have the trumpet sounded loud; on the tenth day of the seventh month—on the day of atonement—you shall have the trumpet sounded throughout all your land. And you shall hallow the fiftieth year and you shall proclaim liberty throughout the land to all its inhabitants. It shall be a jubilee for you...

In this year of jubilee you shall return, every one of you, to your property. When you make a sale to your neighbor or buy from your neighbor, you shall not cheat one another. When you buy from your neighbor, you shall pay only for the number of years since the jubilee; the seller shall charge you only for the remaining crop-years. If the years are more, you shall increase the price, and if the years are fewer, you shall diminish the price; for it is a certain number of harvests that are being sold to you. You shall not cheat one another, but you shall fear your God; for I am the LORD your God. ✛ **LEVITICUS 25:8–10, 13–17**

/////////

70

The development of the cycle of Jubilee years happened very early in the history of Israel. In fact, there were two Jubilees that operated on different cycles. Every seven years, the farmland was to be left uncultivated—a kind of Sabbath rest for the land. It is the other Jubilee, based on a longer cycle, that is referred to in this passage. In the fiftieth year—the year after seven cycles of the shorter Jubilee—land was to revert back to its original owners. Practically speaking, this meant that no farmer could sell his ancestral lands to a wealthy buyer in perpetuity. The most he could do was to lease it until the next Jubilee, with a rent determined by the number of years left before the next Jubilee was to occur.

There was a simple and important reason for this law. The fifty-year Jubilee ensured that the ancestral lands of all of the families who had settled in the Promised Land would stay intact. It prevented, or at least greatly diminished, the possibility that the wealthiest individuals would grow even more wealthy by buying up the lands of the poor. Often the subsistence farmer is forced to sell his land as a result of a poor crop or unanticipated calamity in order to break even, thus making it even harder to make ends meet the next year. Millions of small landowners throughout history have entered into a spiral of poverty this way from which there is no exit except death. In a time when the only really secure wealth was land, such a spiral, if left unchecked, inevitably would result in a society where the vast majority of the wealth was in the hands of a very few and the vast majority of the people would be reduced to indentured servitude or to slavery in every way but the name.

Failure to celebrate the Jubilee, in other words, would result in a society very much like the one that exists in our country, and to a greater extent, the world today. A recent study on global distribution of wealth in the world found that the richest eight people in the world control as much wealth as the poorest three and a half *billion*. While the gap is not quite so large in America, it is still formidable, and growing. Reliable sources report that, in 1979, the wealthiest one percent of Americans controlled about ten percent of the country's wealth. A generation later (2016) they controlled more than twenty percent of the country's wealth. Should that percentage double again in the next generation, how far away will we be from a new feudalism?

The lesson we can derive both from ancient times and from today is obvious. Unless there is a conscious, consistent, and communal effort to create and maintain structures that ensure a more even distribution of wealth, or that from time to time redistribute wealth, an enormous gap will inevitably occur. Increasingly, those on the poorer side of the gap will lack the means to live anything even approaching a decent human life. The rise of the middle class in America was in part brought about by the prosperity generated by a free market economy, but just as much by associations such as unions and the establishment of a social safety net, including Social Security, Medicare, and Medicaid. Such programs temper the excesses of the free market not just by relying on personal generosity but also by creating structures committed to the common good.

Perhaps already you can feel your blood boiling a bit. Isn't this whole idea of limiting commerce and economic growth through the intervention of laws such as the Jubilee in ancient times, or contemporary government programs that rely on taxes, an attack on the American Dream? Don't we all have a right to enjoy every last bit of the fruits of our labor?

From the point of view of Catholic teaching—from the point of view of Jesus—the answer is *no*. The right to private ownership is never absolute. It is always limited by the needs of the poor.

Perhaps Christians could be more accepting of a totally unfettered free market economy if our society was a level playing field and everyone really did have the same shot at prosperity. Any honest study of the history of the United States, however, will reveal that the "level playing field" is, was, and likely always will be a myth. The ancient Hebrews were wise enough to recognize this. So must we.

FOR REFLECTION *and* DISCUSSION

1. When I read this Catholic social justice principle—that the right of private ownership is limited—what is my reaction? Why?

2. What are the structural injustices that exist in our society that contribute to vastly unequal distribution of wealth? What can be done to remedy them?

3. Have I benefited in any way from the lack of a level playing field in society? How? What might I be able to do to help even things out?

4. What sacrifices am I willing to make so that America can become a more just society?

5. As a parish, how would we define the common good? For our community? For ourselves? For our country? For our world?

GOING FORWARD...

In the coming weeks, I/we will identify, denounce, and begin to remedy one particular injustice in our community. The injustice I/we see most clearly is...

I/we will take the following steps to address it...

CLOSING PRAYER

Come Holy Spirit,
fill me with the "hunger and thirst"
    for justice.
Transform my heart so that,
    more and more,
I experience the needs of the poor and the marginalized
    with the same urgency
    as I experience my own needs.
Amen.

Am I a cheerful giver?

The point is this: the one who sows sparingly will also reap sparingly, and the one who sows bountifully will also reap bountifully. Each of you must give as you have made up your mind, not reluctantly or under compulsion, for God loves a cheerful giver. And God is able to provide you with every blessing in abundance, so that by always having enough of everything, you may share abundantly in every good work. As it is written,
  "He scatters abroad, he gives to the poor;
  his righteousness endures forever."

✝ **2 CORINTHIANS 9:6–9**

The first thing that came to mind for me when I reflected upon this reading was an incident that happened while I was on vacation some years ago. A group of Girl Scouts had set up a table selling cookies right in front of the supermarket I was about to enter. At the time I had all the Girl Scout cookies I needed; a few weeks before I bought several boxes from a colleague at work whose daughter was selling them. First, I looked to see if there was another entrance, but there wasn't. These girls had truly scouted out the territory well.

I couldn't bring myself to walk past their smiling little faces exuding cold indifference. Reluctantly, I bought another box of cookies. Technically you could call what I did a kind of charitable giving, but it certainly didn't feel that way. I came away with the strong sense that whatever minuscule amount of good I just did for the world was canceled out by the lingering sense of resentment I felt.

It is the internal disposition toward giving that Paul focuses upon in this reading. It isn't enough simply to give. If we give to charity out of a desire for self-aggrandizement (something that Jesus speaks about in chapter six of the Sermon on the Mount, as well) or mechanically as when we toss a few coins into the beggar's cup so he or she won't bother us, or, as I did, because we have been "guilted into it," something crucial in what should have been a beautiful exchange of love has been lost. While it's true that a large donation to a worthy charity, even if made by a scoundrel seeking to improve his or her public image, can still do much good for the world, it won't do much good for the donor. As St. Teresa of Calcutta said, the ability to "share in the joy of giving" is lost. Given that the donor is integrally connected to the larger community, in some way the community is damaged as well.

What does it mean to give cheerfully? Christian generosity is at its core a free-will, joyful gesture motivated by love. As we become more aware of how much God loves us, we are transformed. We begin to understand that God has the same love for the other person, and our hearts become more and more on fire with the desire to love and to serve those whom we can help. When our desire to give is rooted in this place, we give the needy person or group much more than our material resources. We communicate to them a sense that they are honored and cherished. We are then participating in a relationship that is the definitive experience of life in the Kingdom. The joy we receive makes us aware that we get as much as we give when we do so cheerfully.

Three examples come to mind that illustrate well what Paul is preaching. I once read an editorial in a New York paper that suggested rather than mindlessly throwing a few coins in the beggar's cup, try looking into the person's eyes for a moment and saying a prayer for him or her. On the few occasions I have felt comfortable enough to do this, I seem to be able to actually catch a glimpse of the person's humanity. It is much harder to disregard a person for whom you have prayed.

The second example comes from the ministry of St. Teresa of Calcutta. The ministry of the Missionaries of Charity, the religious order St. Teresa founded, began with the gathering up of beggars dying on the streets of Calcutta. These beggars were close to death and beyond any hope of physical recovery. Motivated by love and not by any human desire for accomplishment, St. Teresa and her sisters understood that they had an opportunity to provide these forgotten children of God with a place to die with dignity, so that at least in their final hours they might become aware of what had always been true—how precious they were in God's eyes.

While most of us will never find ourselves in extreme situations such as those within which St. Teresa lived out her ministry, all of us have opportunities to help repair the dignity of one who has suffered the sometimes brutal realities of daily life. When we comfort our children after a tough day at school, when we make a point of checking in with the coworker who was chewed out by the boss earlier in the day, when we volunteer for a community cleanup drive to make our neighborhoods seem a bit cheerier and more livable, we are doing in a small but real way what St. Teresa sought to do in Calcutta.

Finally, the prophet Micah, reflecting upon the essence of covenant, tells us that three things are necessary to live in relationship with God, with others, and with creation: "Do good, love righteousness, walk humbly with God" (Micah 6:8). Only the first requirement applies to outward actions—another way of expressing Jesus' teaching that, "by their fruits, you will know them." The other two apply to what is happening within our hearts. Does the good we do flow out of a genuine desire to serve others? Is giving so natural that we can truly say with Jesus that our "left hand does not know what our right hand is doing" because generosity has become a way of life? And, finally, are we consciously aware that all of the good we do is actually not ours at all but brought to fruition by the love of God flowing through us?

God loves a cheerful giver. And, more and more, the cheerful giver discovers within himself or herself a passionate love for God.

FOR REFLECTION *and* DISCUSSION

1. Have I ever shared my time, talents, and treasure more out of a sense of obligation than out of a conscious and free-will choice? How was the experience different from times I was a cheerful giver?

2. Reflect upon a time when you truly were a cheerful giver. What was the result? What change resulted?

3. In what areas of my life do I find it natural and easy to be a cheerful giver? Where is it difficult? Why?

4. Can I recall a recent encounter in which I was able to catch a glimpse of the presence of God in that person? Can I recall an encounter in which I could not overcome my basic antipathy, ambivalence, or indifference toward the other person?

5. What is my most powerful experience of being the recipient of the services of a cheerful giver? How did the experience make me feel? How did it change me?

6. As a parish, how many of our ministries are done with joy? Where are the conflicts? Could any of these conflicts be traced to lingering resentments—either among the participants or directed toward those we serve? What would we have to do to resolve these conflicts?

GOING FORWARD...

In this coming week, I/we will pray for _____ , a group/ person I/we usually find it difficult to pray for.

My/Our particular intention will be...

One concrete thing I/we will do for this person/group is...

CLOSING PRAYER

Come, Holy Spirit,
fill my heart
  with a desire to serve.
May my acts
    of generosity
be abundant,
  consistent,
  and cheerful.
Amen.

Am I "the man" (or "the woman")?

The LORD sent Nathan to David. He came to him, and said to him, "There were two men in a certain city, one rich and the other poor. The rich man had very many flocks and herds; but the poor man had nothing but one little ewe lamb, which he had bought. He brought it up, and it grew up with him and with his children; it used to eat of his meager fare, and drink from his cup, and lie in his bosom, and it was like a daughter to him. Now there came a traveler to the rich man, and he was loath to take one of his own flock or herd to prepare for the wayfarer who had come to him, but he took the poor man's lamb, and prepared that for the guest who had come to him." Then David's anger was greatly kindled against the man. He said to Nathan, "As the LORD lives, the man who has done this deserves to die; he shall restore the lamb fourfold, because he did this thing, and because he had no pity."

Nathan said to David, "You are the man!"

✝ **2 SAMUEL 12:1–9**

This confrontation between the prophet Nathan and King David is the dramatic climax of one of the most riveting stories in the Bible. As the story opens, King David is home alone in Jerusalem while all of the men of Israel are away fighting in a battle. David lusts after Bathsheba, the wife of one of his loyal officers named Uriah, and summons her to his palace. She is not given any choice in the matter. A short time later, she informs David that she is pregnant with his child. Now David has a problem. Given that Uriah is off fighting, it is only a matter of time before his adultery becomes known.

Determined to avoid scandal, he hatches a plan. On the pretext of needing more information about how the battle is going, David sends a message to Uriah to come to the palace for a short visit. After receiving his report, David encourages Uriah to spend a few days at home with Bathsheba—which will provide a good cover story to explain how Bathsheba became pregnant while her husband was away for months fighting a battle.

Uriah, however, is everything that David is not. He is loyal and honorable and refuses to abandon his post. He will guard the king until he must return to the front lines. Even David's attempts to get Uriah drunk do not work. Desperate and panic-stricken, David adds murder to his sin of adultery. Taking advantage of Uriah's loyalty, David entrusts him with a sealed note to be delivered to Jabeth, the general of the army. The note contains only one directive: Jabeth is to place Uriah in the front lines during the battle and then order the rest of his troops to pull back. The general does as he is told, Uriah dies in battle, and after waiting for a suitable period of mourning, David takes the widow Bathsheba into his harem where she can be hidden away until the child is born.

It's at this point in the story that David receives a visit from his advisor, the prophet Nathan, who tells the tale about the rich man who stole the poor man's lamb. It would have initially appeared to King David that Nathan was asking him to pronounce judgment on a court case involving some nobleman of the realm, a common practice of the time. In fact, Nathan was actually telling a parable designed to catch David off guard and make him understand the terrible injustice he had committed. Thus, the dramatic moment: "You are the man!"

This parable does more than wake David up, however. It also gets to the root of what caused both the adultery and the murder. The king lacks any sense of the common good; he simply assumes that, because he is king, everything he desires belongs to him. This monstrous sense of entitlement was not unique to David. It is all too common among the rich and powerful, both then and now. It is an attitude of the heart that turns the Catholic social justice principle of the common good—that all of the economic, political, and social decisions we make should be primarily concerned with what is best for all in society, not what is best for us—on its head. For David and those of his ilk, the common good is invariably, and erroneously, equated with their personal good.

The size and scope of both David's sins and power are, of course, extraordinary. Yet if we honestly search our hearts, we may find we are not all that different from David. Each time we take questionable legal and moral steps in order to avoid paying our fair share of taxes, or seek only the cheapest price for the products we purchase regardless of whether or not those products were manufactured by an overworked and underpaid labor force somewhere in the world, or turn a blind eye to business practices in our places of employment that put profits over a responsibility to the community, or vote for candidates who promise to advance our financial prospects and security without regard for the poor and the vulnerable, we are choosing our personal good over the common good.

There is a hopeful epilogue to the story. When David's sins are placed before him so clearly, he repents. He falls to his knees in prayer and, upon rising, begins to change into a better man. When we who are blessed with abundance are confronted with our sins against the common good, how do we react?

FOR REFLECTION *and* DISCUSSION

1. Have I ever taken something that was not mine? Why?

2. Have I, am I, struggling with the sin of envy? Be as specific as you can be.

3. In what area of my life has self-centeredness affected my sense of justice?

4. How would I define the difference between wants and needs? Have I ever confused the two?

5. On a scale of 1 to 10, how much effort do we as a parish put into trying to find out how socially responsible the companies are with which we do business? Do we even see this as our responsibility to work with vendors committed to the common good? Are business decisions in the parish based more on nepotism, bargain prices, and/or inertia? Finally, is it always a practice of good stewardship to take the lowest bid on a proposed project?

GOING FORWARD...

This week I/we will investigate the commitment to the common good of this particular company with whom I/we do much business...

The behavior that I/we would expect from a socially responsible business would be...

If I/we find out that a company with which we do business is acting in a socially irresponsible way, I/we will...

CLOSING PRAYER

Loving God,
You provide me with all that I need.
You have blessed me with abundance.
Create in me a clean heart.
Help me to discern the difference
    between wants and needs.
Teach me to share.
Remind me
        again and again
    of my responsibility
to provide as best I can
    for the needs of the poor.
Amen.

Do I use the goods of this world to advance the Kingdom?

Then Jesus said to the disciples, "There was a rich man who had a manager, and charges were brought to him that this man was squandering his property. So he summoned him and said to him, 'What is this that I hear about you? Give me an account of your management, because you cannot be my manager any longer.' Then the manager said to himself, 'What will I do, now that my master is taking the position away from me? I am not strong enough to dig, and I am ashamed to beg. I have decided what to do so that, when I am dismissed as manager, people may welcome me into their homes.' So, summoning his master's debtors one by one, he asked the first, 'How much do you owe my master?' He answered, 'A hundred jugs of olive oil.' He said to him, 'Take your bill, sit down quickly, and make it fifty.' Then he asked another, 'And how much do you owe?' He replied, 'A hundred containers of wheat.' He said to him, 'Take your bill and make it eighty.' And his master commended the dishonest manager because he had acted shrewdly; for the children of this age are more shrewd in dealing with their own generation than are the children of light." ✝ LUKE 16:1–8

"Be wise as serpents but innocent as doves." ✝ MATTHEW 10:16

If this story were found in Machiavelli's *The Prince* or in a new edition of Dale Carnegie's *How to Win Friends and Influence People*, we would not be surprised. But what do we make of it as it comes from the mouth of Jesus?

It appears at first glance that Jesus is complementing the manager for his dishonest behavior. This is hard to understand, because not only did the servant "squander" the rich man's property—perhaps by embezzlement—but he has now hatched a plot to deliberately misrepresent the rightful debts due to his master to create a softer landing for himself. Knowing that he is "not strong enough to dig and ashamed to beg," he attempts to create a reservoir of good will to tide him over until he can find a new position.

Can we, perhaps, justify the dishonest steward's behavior as a kind of "Robin Hood" mission—robbing from his rich master so that he can ease the burden of poverty among his debtors? Certainly, the inequalities between rich and poor and the vicious cycle of poverty were as real in Jesus' time as they are now. Such an interpretation is possible, but nothing in the story as Jesus tells it suggests that this steward is motivated by anything but pure, unadulterated self-interest. He is a survivor whose philosophy seems to be, "Look out for Number One."

The key to understanding why Jesus offers the dishonest servant to his disciples for their consideration is found in the second short passage from Matthew's gospel. In this unrelated account taken from Jesus' ministry, Jesus exhorts his disciples to be "as wise as serpents and as innocent [or, in other translations, harmless] as doves." Jesus is not admiring the servant's dishonesty. It is his determination that Jesus wishes his disciples to reflect upon. Faced with his personal ruin, the dishonest servant is focused on only one thing: What do I need to do to survive? Given that motivation, Jesus suggests, his plan is rather ingenious. He is a good example of the "wise serpent," understood in this context as an individual who is crafty enough to make a system that is designed to exclude or to diminish him work instead in his favor.

Where the dishonest servant comes up short, obviously, is when we consider the "innocent as doves" part of Jesus' exhortation. Clearly, he isn't innocent at all. Yet imagine what he could have accomplished if his motives were more generous. There are a number of examples we can point to in the history of the church of people who were able to hold together both parts of Jesus' statement and transform, not necessarily their own personal prospects, but society and the church for the better.

St. Paul wisely figured out how to present the gospel, rooted in a very unique interpretation of Jewish messianism, in a way that would be intelligible to a much wider Gentile audience. St. Francis and St. Clare wisely understood that the church's outreach to the poor in a society that was transitioning from feudal estates to commerce centered in towns required a new approach. Their God-given creativity and ingenuity resulted in the beginnings of the mendicant religious orders that lived among the poor ("mendicant" means "beggar") in order to better serve them. In modern times, Dorothy Day was wise enough to see through the whole "dirty rotten system" of American politics and capitalism, which almost always favors the rich at the expense of the poor and, increasingly, fosters a "military-industrial complex" that swallows an ever-larger percentage of resources in the pursuit of more and more horrifyingly powerful weapons. With the help and guidance of a number of other equally creative and ingenious souls, she brought into being a multi-prong approach to transforming culture that provided for the immediate needs of the poor through Houses of Hospitality, did important consciousness raising among American society at large through the publication of the *Catholic Worker*, and organized protests highlighting the insanity of the military industrial complex.

Considering these examples, how does this generation of Christian disciples measure up? Are we as wise as serpents when it comes to finding new and creative ways to share our abundance with the poor and influencing the culture we live in to ensure that resources are more equitably distributed and injustice reduced? Do our creativity and ingenuity match that of the dishonest servant, not when it comes to advancing our own self-interest, but in advancing the interests of the common good and the Kingdom of God? We might look at actor Paul Newman, whose successful "Newman's Own" brand of products donates all its profits to charity, as an example. Or to Bill and Melinda Gates, whose commitment to charitable giving is not simply a hobby or a tax write-off but an integral part of their lives. Perhaps we can take our inspiration from those more anonymous (though not to God) individuals who, through the helping professions or through innovative business operations, have found new and creative ways to serve the common good, sometimes at great personal sacrifice.

The "wisdom of serpents" and the "innocence of doves" can be found in the church as well. Organizations of the laity such as Pax Christi or the Voice of the Faithful or Fr. Greg Boyle's creative adaptation of his priestly ministry in the form of Homeboy Industries, a business enterprise aimed at removing young men from gangs and giving them gainful employment, are all examples of how creative and committed people can work within the world to change the world.

While some of these examples may not resonate, as they require wealth and fame beyond ours, it is important to keep in mind that

God's measuring stick is always relative. It isn't so much about how much we do, or how much we give, that matters. As St. Teresa often said, it is about "how much of ourselves we put into the doing." As we go about our daily economic and social lives, are we at least as determined to do what we can to advance the Kingdom of God in the here and now as we are about advancing our own prospects? Or, like the dishonest servant, are we squandering the creativity and ingenuity God has blessed us with for our own selfish ends?

When, like the dishonest steward, we seek creative ways to take control of our wealth and our economic decisions but, unlike the steward, we seek to do so for the benefit of the community, the possibilities are endless.

FOR REFLECTION *and* DISCUSSION

1. What are some of the creative and generous ways I have used my wealth to benefit those outside of my immediate circle of family and friends?

2. What are some ways within my place of employment that I can foster and build a climate in which service to the community is as important as making a profit?

3. What is the balance like for me between the creativity and energy I put into earning a living and the creativity and energy I put into using my wealth to make meaningful changes in my community and the greater society? What is one thing I could do to shift the balance a bit toward justice?

4. What are the ways that I help to build community? What is my motivation? What are some creative and innovative ways I might follow to deepen community in my parish and neighborhood?

5. As a parish, what are some ways we can transform our parish life so that, like Dorothy Day, we provide for the immediate needs of the poor, raise the consciousness of our parishioners, and creatively and persistently engage in prayerful and meaningful dialogue with the greater society concerning the common good?

GOING FORWARD…

In this coming week, I/we will seek to be "wise as serpents and innocent as doves" by creatively seeking to redirect wealth or by using resources more efficiently for the greater good of society in the following way…

Several signs that would indicate to me/us that our plan is working would be…

CLOSING PRAYER

Lord Jesus, you call us to be
*   wise as serpents but innocent as doves.*
Send your Spirit to set our hearts
*   and our imaginations on fire.*
Help us to see possibilities for change
*   and even transformation in ourselves,*
*   in our society, and in our church*
*   that we have not been able to see before.*
Through the generous and creative use
*   of our time, talent, and treasure,*
may we transform the world into a more perfect likeness
*   of your Kingdom.*
Amen.

Do I "pray away" my obligation to the poor?

What good is it, my brothers and sisters, if you say you have faith but do not have works? Can faith save you? If a brother or sister is naked and lacks daily food, and one of you says to them, "Go in peace; keep warm and eat your fill," and yet you do not supply their bodily needs, what is the good of that? So faith by itself, if it has no works, is dead. ✛ JAMES 2:14–17

~~~~~~~~~

Every day, at the beginning of each class I teach, we pray for special intentions. Sometimes it is for the particular needs of my students, sometimes for the needs of the school, often for the needs of the poor in our city, our country, and our world. That's five classes a day times about one hundred and eighty days. Add to that every other Catholic school teacher who does the same thing plus all of the intentions for the poor we offer when we pray at the start or close of the day; and combine those prayers with the prayers of all of the faithful offered during the celebration of the Eucharist on Sunday. We don't even have to consider the many other formal and informal prayers said by millions of people every day to realize that our prayers for those in need are as numberless as the grains of sand on the beach or the stars in the heavens.

Of course, it is good that we do this. Prayer, particularly when it is offered on behalf of others, transforms us. It raises our minds and hearts to a greater awareness of and experience within that web of relationships that unites all humans brought into being through Christ by the power of God's love. For a moment at least, our consciousness is reoriented as we place the needs of others above our own. Our prayers resonate through the sacred chords that connect us all.

It is important, however, that we take a moment to think about the manner and means by which our prayers on behalf of the poor are often answered. Or, at least, the way God wishes to answer them. God responds not through miraculous interventions that suspend the known laws of physics, but through a power even more impressive than that which parted the Red Sea. God intends to answer those prayers on behalf of the poor through the love, compassion, and efforts of his disciples who make up the church. More often than we realize, God hears our prayers, desires quite deeply that they be answered, and provides the means by which they can be answered: us.

Shane Claibourne tells the story explaining his own transformation from seminary student to embracing a Franciscan-like ministry among the poorest of the poor. One morning during breakfast, one of his fellow seminarians threw a newspaper down on the table. On the page displayed was a story about a group of homeless families in Philadelphia who had found refuge in an abandoned church but were about to be evicted for trespassing. His heart filled with compassion as well as outrage at the irony of the situation. Claibourne says he became angry with God in prayer and called out, "Why don't you do something!" In the stillness that followed, the answer to his question resonated clearly within his soul. "I did do something," God seemed to be saying. "I made you. Go to Philadelphia!" Thus began a mission among the poor that Claiborne writes about in great detail in his book *The Irresistible Revolution*.

The way that God answers prayers—or sometimes seems not to answer—can be hard to fathom. There is one prayer, however, to which God's answer will be clear, concise, and immediate. If we pray for the grace to see those today whom we can help and for the love we need to move into action, God will be eager to respond. To simply pray for the poor as a matter of habit without a determination to help is to be the person whom St. James describes in his letter—the person who says to his or her brother or sister in need, "Go in peace, keep warm, and eat your fill" but who does nothing to make this possible. If our prayers for the poor result in no increase in our own generosity or compassion, they are not prayers at all. They are fruitless. What we thought was an expression of a faith burning brightly, St. James soberly states, is in fact dying embers. Only when we allow the Spirit, as Shane Claiborne did, to transform our good intentions into action can we be sure our faith is burning as brightly as we think it is.

Faith without works is dead. Prayer without action is impotent. At this very moment, what is God calling you do to with the blessings you have received? To whom might the Spirit be sending you?

FOR REFLECTION *and* **DISCUSSION**

1. Whose needs—material and spiritual—is God sending me to meet today?

2. When it comes to what I do with my wealth, is there a disconnect between what I say and what I believe? Between what I believe and what I do? Why does this disconnect exist?

3. Do my choices at the ballot box reflect the social justice principles of the church? What am I doing in my role as a citizen to help create a more just society, especially for the poor?

4. How often do I pray for the poor? Have I ever begun the day asking God to show me the needs of the poor I might meet today? Why or why not?

5. When as a parish we pray to God for guidance on how to help the poor, what ideas come to mind? Upon how many of those ideas have we acted? Who are the prophets among us calling us to action?

GOING FORWARD...

I/we believe that at this time God is calling us to do the following in order to help the poor...

I/we can begin to answer this call by taking the following steps...

CLOSING PRAYER

Jesus,
you hold the poor
   so closely
     in your heart.
Throughout the centuries
   you have called upon your church
   to meet the needs of the poor
     through both traditional and innovative ways.
Show us the most pressing needs
     of our time.
Send your Spirit
   upon us,
that we might have
   the compassion,
   the wisdom,
     and the determination we need
   to be your hands
     in meeting those needs.
Finally, increase our faith
   in the belief that
     even when it seems our prayers fall to the ground in tatters
   you are always there to mend them together again.
Amen.

Am I letting my desire for material gain destroy my Sabbath?

Remember the sabbath day, and keep it holy. For six days you shall labor and do all your work. But the seventh day is a sabbath to the LORD your God; you shall not do any work— you, your son or your daughter, your male or female slave, your livestock, or the alien resident in your towns. For in six days the LORD made heaven and earth, the sea, and all that is in them, but rested the seventh day; therefore the LORD blessed the sabbath day and consecrated it. + **EXODUS 20:8–11**

~~~~~~~~~

What does it mean to keep holy the Sabbath? The answer seems obvious to any Catholic who has attained the age of reason. We are to go to church on Sunday and participate fully in the celebration of the Eucharist. This sacred experience is identified by the Second Vatican Council as the "source and summit" of our Christian faith.

Certainly, setting aside time to worship God together as a community is essential, yet it is not the *fullness* of observing the Sabbath and keeping it holy.

As the Scripture passage from the book of Exodus indicates, the importance of observing the Sabbath by gathering together for prayer and worship has ancient roots. The majority of the psalms, for example, were originally written in connection with the Temple worship of the people of Judah who would make pilgrimages to Jerusalem to pray together as often as possible, but certainly during the Passover festival. When the Temple was destroyed by the Roman army in 70 AD, many more Jews were added to the diaspora (Jewish communities scattered throughout the Roman Empire). For these refugees, as well as for thousands of other Jews, praying together in the synagogue increasingly became the focal point of their communal Sabbath prayer. When the church and the synagogue went their separate ways, the custom of keeping holy the Sabbath through community worship was, therefore, already well entrenched.

What did not become so well entrenched among Christians, however, was the *reason* God set aside the Sabbath as holy. According to the book of Genesis, God created the Sabbath so that God might celebrate all of the beauty and wonder of creation. The implication of the story is: If God was not too busy to take time off and appreciate life, how can we honestly believe that we are too busy? Could it possibly be that we think our work is more important than God's? In the movie *Ferris Bueller's Day Off*, the title character puts it this way: "Life moves pretty fast. If you don't stop and look around once in a while, you could miss it."

Intuitively, at the core of our souls, we Catholics know this. We recognize that absolutely everything that God created—the natural world, other people, ourselves, and the sacred interweaving of all of the people, places, and events of our lives within our hearts and minds that we call memory—reflects the loving imagination and providence of the Creator. Sin has taken its toll, and we continue to grapple with its effects—but while sin can taint, it cannot destroy. This implicit desire not just to worship God within the world but *through* the world is what makes us a sacramental people.

In order for us to appreciate as fully as we possibly can the unique graces that flow from Christ through the seven sacraments of the church, we must become ever more fully aware of the sacramental nature of our lives. To say that something is sacramental is to proclaim, as Julian of Norwich said of a simple hazelnut, that "God made it, God keeps it, and God loves it."

In fact, it is precisely because sin has dimmed our vision of the glory surrounding us that we need to consciously take time to appreciate what is good and what is beautiful on a regular basis. To "recreate," in the truest sense of the word, is to experience again the newness and wonder of life we first experienced as children. To take time to spend with those we love, to engage in hobbies and activities that feed our hearts and minds and souls, whether that be reading a good book, taking a hike, or going rollerblading, is to praise God. When, in conjunction with full, active, and conscious participation in the Eucharist, we keep holy the Sabbath in this way, we allow the Spirit to refresh our hearts and our minds and our souls so that we might remember what an incredible, unique gift our lives are. Such a sabbath observance cannot help but exude holiness.

We live in a culture that is constantly bombarding us with two lies from the Father of Lies: 1) Happiness lies in the accumulation of wealth and 2) Our self-worth is connected to the wealth we generate. Adding to our stress, the mechanistic operation of our free market system leaves increasing numbers of people one paycheck away from economic ruin and homelessness. The very thought of leisure time is considered by many to be the height of vanity. (Please understand—I am not referring here to those struggling millions who have all they can do to make ends meet on a minimum wage. Their inability to enjoy leisure time is more the fault of our failure as a society as a whole—and as a church—to insist that the right to work include more than a job but must also include a living wage. And to understand that a living wage does not just mean the ability to provide food, clothing, and shelter, but to provide for one's family all that is necessary to live a fully human life.) How crucial it is, therefore, to use our celebration of the Sabbath as a constant reminder that "God knows we need these things" and that six days are plenty of time to do what we must to provide for the material needs of ourselves and our families.

How do you honor the Sabbath? When you participate in the celebration of the Eucharist (literally, the "celebration of thanksgiving") on Sunday, what are you giving thanks for? In what ways do you see the presence of the risen Christ in your life? The flower of eternal joy in the Kingdom of God only blooms if it is rooted in a sense of gratitude and awe for the goodness of God in this life that is made real in the experience of true Sabbath. Such an experience can only occur when we allow the time and space in our lives for genuine leisure.

FOR REFLECTION AND DISCUSSION

1. Besides going to Mass on Sunday, how do I keep the Sabbath?

2. Jesus said that "The Sabbath was made for humankind, and not humankind for the Sabbath." What does this mean to me?

3. Do I have a healthy balance between work and leisure in my life? If yes, how do I maintain it? If no, what must I change in order to strike a healthier balance?

4. When I take a few quiet moments to count my blessings, which ones do I become most aware of?

5. Do we as a parish staff and/or as a parish community make time to get to know one another through leisure activities? What are some ways as a community we could work to involve more parishioners in the daily life of the parish? Are those of us most active in ministry responding to a call from Jesus exclusively or are we sometimes responding to the call of our own egos (the voice that says, "I am irreplaceable," or that says, "My worth is defined by my accomplishments")?

GOING FORWARD...

In order to more fully celebrate the Sabbath in the coming weeks, I / we will make time for the following activities and people... (Feel free to combine both lists. For example: "Go to a movie with my brother and sister.")

CLOSING PRAYER

Heavenly Father and Mother,
I am so grateful for all the blessings
you have bestowed upon me.
Grant me the grace of the Spirit
to truly see your presence in all the people,
in all the places, and in all the events of my life.
May I keep holy the Sabbath
not only in a joyful celebration of the Eucharist
but in a joyful celebration of my life.
May my Sabbath joy be palpable and infectious
as it emanates from me to every person I meet.
Amen.

Am I building a legacy
or a useless tower?

Now the whole earth had one language and the same words.…
Then they said, "Come, let us build ourselves a city, and a tower
with its top in the heavens, and let us make a name for ourselves;
otherwise we shall be scattered abroad upon the face of the whole
earth." The LORD came down to see the city and the tower, which
mortals had built. And the LORD said, "Look, they are one people,
and they have all one language; and this is only the beginning
of what they will do; nothing that they propose to do will now
be impossible for them. Come, let us go down, and confuse their
language there, so that they will not understand one another's
speech." So the LORD scattered them abroad from there over the
face of all the earth, and they left off building the city. Therefore it
was called Babel, because there the LORD confused the language
of all the earth; and from there the LORD scattered them abroad
over the face of all the earth. ✣ GENESIS 11:1, 4–9

~~~~~~~~~

"You can't take it with you." Everyone knows this. Whatever wealth
and power and fame we have accumulated will belong to someone

else after we die. If we are fortunate enough to have enough left over after our final bills are paid to leave our children an inheritance, or perhaps to donate to a worthy charity, we can have some say about how our wealth will be used after we are gone. Only for a while, however.

Every so often, archaeologists somewhere in the world uncover an ancient tomb containing great wealth. Such a tomb provides unmistakable evidence that a rich and powerful individual was buried there. Likely he or she was a respected leader or warrior known and loved—or at least feared—by all. We can see breathtakingly beautiful examples of these grave goods in any major museum of the world. With few exceptions, however, the identity of the occupant of the tomb has been lost to history. Like those who labored upon the Tower of Babel, attempting to build a name for themselves that would outlast even God, these dignitaries of former times found that despite their best efforts their desire to be eternally remembered was ultimately frustrated. If this is true for the wealthiest and most powerful human beings, how much more is it true for the rest of us!

This raises an important question: What makes for a lasting legacy? We have recognized in several meditations in this book that while material wealth can be placed in the service of the Kingdom of God, it cannot get us there. In fact, if we hold on to our wealth too tightly, it becomes an impediment. While we believe confidently in St. Paul's proclamation that "eye has not seen and ear has not heard what God has ready for those who love him," our inability to grasp the warp and the weft of eternal life tempts us again and again to cling to the more tangible achievements and comforts of this life.

"Faith, hope, and love remain, these three, but the greatest of these is love." These words, written by St. Paul almost two thousand years ago, remind us of what the builders of the Tower of Babel forgot. If we truly seek to build an eternal legacy, we need to make use of the spiritual bricks and mortar supplied by the Holy Spirit.

Through *faith*, we can let go of the things of this world and place our trust in God. Gradually, we learn to tell the difference between "who we are" and "what we have." *Hope* gives us the energy to build upon the spiritual foundations Christ laid down through his life, death, and resurrection; it is the virtue that enables us to see the completed Kingdom even while we labor in the already/not yet of the present moment.

Finally, *love* is the mortar that holds the entire structure of our lives, the church, and all of creation together. It never cracks, never needs to be replaced, never shrinks, always grows. Love is the only thing that is truly eternal because it is the essence of the Trinity. It is through love that we become what we were always intended to be—children of God.

Ralph Waldo Emerson offered a description of what such a legacy might look like in his poem entitled, "Success":

> *To laugh often and much,*
> *to win respect of intelligent people*
> *and the affection of children;*
> *to earn the appreciation of honest critics*
> *and endure the betrayal of false friends;*
> *to appreciate beauty;*
> *to find the best in others;*
> *to leave the world a bit better whether by*
> *a healthy child, a garden patch,*
> *or a redeemed social condition;*
> *to know even one life has breathed*

easier because you have lived.
This is to have succeeded.

What all of the meditations in this book come down to is one simple truth: When we decide to hand over the construction of our lives to the Master Builder, when we recognize that whatever material wealth we have been given—which is often more than we realize—is a gift from God to us to be shared with others for the purpose of building up the Kingdom, we begin to understand what Jesus meant in a series of brief parables he used to describe that reality. That "pearl of great price" will never be found in any marketplace. It will always be found where God has placed it—in the very center of our hearts.

FOR REFLECTION AND DISCUSSION

1. What kind of a legacy am I building? How much of it is dependent on wealth?

2. Who are the people I most admire in my life? Why? (Consider both the living and the dead, the famous and those known personally by you.)

3. How do I see faith, hope and love manifested in my life at this moment?

4. How would I like to be remembered? (Be as specific as possible. If you are comfortable doing so, you might even want to write out your own imaginary obituary.)

5. If as a parish we were to craft our own definition of "Success," what would it say? What are the specific signs we can point to,

or would like to be able to point to, that would affirm for us we were in fact following the call of the Spirit and serving the people of God in the parish? (Be as specific as you can here.)

GOING FORWARD...

I/We will take the following steps to leave a lasting legacy of meaning for my/our community...

CLOSING PRAYER

Thank you, Father and Mother,
for this precious gift of life.
Each day,
show me how to make the most
of the resources you have placed
at my disposal.
Most of all,
lead me by the way
of love,
so that I might use all my energies
and powers
and wealth
to transform the world
more and more
into the image of your Kingdom.
Amen.

SUGGESTED METHOD FOR USING THESE
MEDITATIONS IN A **GROUP SETTING**

This outline assumes a one-hour time of prayer and reflection.

Begin, if necessary, by having everyone introduce themselves.

Allow a few minutes for a brief quieting exercise.
(Simply beginning with a few deep breaths in silence would be fine.)

Read the Scripture passage slowly and prayerfully.

Pause

Read all or part of the reflection.
*(It is advisable for you as the leader to read over the meditation
ahead of time and to perhaps highlight those parts of the
reflection that seem important. When the meditation begins,
however, let the Holy Spirit take precedence over your notes!)*

Allow ten or fifteen minutes for private, silent reflection.
*(You might wish to provide pencils and paper so participants can
jot down a few thoughts.)*

Spend about twenty minutes in faith sharing as a group.
*(You might want to focus on one question or allow the group
to determine the focus. Probably it is best not to try and deal
with all the questions. Keep in mind the advisory given in the
Introduction about managing tensions that may arise.)*

Allow fifteen minutes for the Going Forward exercise.
(This is the most immediate fruit of the meditation.)

End with the Closing Prayer.